Taboos of Present-day Japan: The Exquisite Subtleness of Being

Tsuchiya Haruhito

装　　幀＝寄藤文平、吉田孝宏
本文イラスト＝斉藤啓（ブッダプロダクションズ）
翻　　訳＝佐藤和枝

現代日本のタブー

その余りにもビミョーな存在

Taboos of Present-day Japan: The Exquisite Subtleness of Being

Tsuchiya Haruhito
土屋晴仁＝著

はじめに

2013年制作のフランスのB級アクション映画『パリ・カウントダウン』(Paris countdown)で、主人公がカネに困ってギャングのボスを訪ねるシーンがある。日本食レストランでボスは寿司を食いながら、主人公にもすすめるが、彼が「生魚はちょっと……」と**尻込み**するのを見てこう言う。

「日本文化なんて、お前らにはあまりにもビミョーだからな」。英語の字幕には「Japanese culture is too subtle for you」と出る。この「subtle」という形容詞は、「微妙な、とらえがたい、名状しがたい」などの意味になる。実は、これこそ「現代ニッポンのタブー」を語るキーワードなのである。

本書はタブーを定義したり、学者めいた**文化論**を語ったりする難しい本ではない。また日本文化に知識も敬意を持たない若者やガイジンが冒す間抜けな言動を**揶揄する**ものでもない。

本書は、現代の日本人自身でさえ気づいていない、しかし確実に生活場面での言動を制約している、みえにくい何らかの「**拘束力**」を観察し、考察してみたいのだ。いや、たいしたことではない。

たとえば、麺類を食べる時、日本人は「ズズーッ」とすすり、音を立てて食べる。自分がそうするだけでなく、来日したガイジンにラーメンやそばをすすめる際に、「**郷に入らば、郷に従え**」で「すすって食べろ」と強要する日本人がいる。しかしア

INTRODUCTION

In a scene of a 2013 French action movie *Paris countdown (Le jour attendra)*, Milan and Victor, the main characters, visit their gang boss at a Japanese restaurant to repay their debts. The boss is there eating sushi, and he offers some to them. But Milan is **hesitant** and says, "I'm not so crazy about raw fish."

The English subtitle reads, "Well, Japanese culture is too subtle for you." The word "subtle" means delicate, complex or difficult to describe. This is a keyword to explain the taboos in present-day Japan.

I'm not trying to define a taboo or talk about an academic, **cultural theory** in this book. Also, it is not my intention to **criticize** young people or *gaijin* (foreigners) who don't have any knowledge or respect for the Japanese culture and do silly things out of ignorance.

What I'd like to do here is to observe and analyze the "**restrictions**" that the Japanese people are not aware of, but they indeed exist and are controlling their lives. It can be seen on many occasions in everyday life.

Let me give you an example: when eating noodles, Japanese "slurp" them with sound. Some people even force *gaijin* to do the same insisting, "**In Rome, do as the Romans do**." But most of the foreigners, including

ジア圏を含むほとんどのガイジンは、そうすることを生理的に嫌う。幼い時からしつけられているからだ。

慣れない行為に「No!」と言う人に、何かを押し付けるのは少しも「おもてなし」ではない。犯罪に近い。だからこの行為に対して、「ヌーハラ」(ヌードル・ハラスメント)という言葉も生まれてしまった。日本人はこれからも麺類をすすって食べ続けるだろう。そしてガイジンは「No!」と言い続けるだろう。どこまでも交わらない、この些細な文化上の「タブー」はいったいどうして生まれ、どう変化するものだろう……?そんなレベルのことを考えてみたいのである。

本書は、身の回りにたくさんあるこうした事象を観察し、考察する本である。そう、決してハイブロウ(highbrow)ではない。もし、本書を手にして、ジェームズ・フレーザー卿の『金枝篇』(The Golden Bough)や、日本の**民俗学者**・柳田国男の『禁忌習俗事典』を現代ニッポンに適用して解説したものか、と期待したのなら、そっと書棚に戻していただく方が良いだろう。

私がこだわるのはやはり「subtle」な、タブーとそうでないものとの**境界線**である。ある人にとっては「No!」なのに、別の人には「Yes!」であるとか、ある場合には右なのに、別の場合には左とか、昔は多くの人が従っていたのに今ではごく少数しか従わないなど……、その違いを誰も明確に、科学的に、合理的に説明はできない。しかし現実にそういう事象が発生している現場に興味があるのだ。なぜなら、人生も世界も不合

the ones from Asian countries, simply can't do it because it's against the manners they've been taught by their parents.

Forcing someone to do something that **he or she is not used to doing** is not *omotenashi* (hospitality) at all. It is almost a crime. For this kind of behavior, a word *noo-hara* (noodle harassment) was created. The Japanese will continue to slurp noodles, and *gaijin* will keep on saying "No!" to that, and this will not change. How was this kind of minor cultural "taboo" born? Will it ever change? These are the kind of things that I'd like to think about here.

This book aims to observe and study those taboos around us. It is not intended to be a highbrow book. If you expect something like "The Golden Bough" by James Fraser or a contemporary version of *Kinki shūzoku jiten* [Taboos and customs dictionary] by Kunio Yanagita, a Japanese **folklorist**, you came to the wrong place. Just put this book back on the shelf at the bookstore.

What I stick with is the "subtle" **borderline** between the taboos: a taboo that is OK for some but not for others; right in one case but left in another; old popular rituals that became minor, etc. Nobody could explain those differences clearly, scientifically, and rationally. But I'm interested in the scenes where the taboos can be seen. Our lives and the world are filled with irrational

理なことの連続で、曖昧なことだらけではないか。だからこそ面白くてエキサイティングだ。もし、これが何から何までクリアで、正義と不正義がはっきり区分され、**明日の暮らしも計算ずくめ**だとしたら、生きるに値しない。

日本ほど、「subtle」なタブーに囲まれている社会はないと思う。だからこそ、私はこの国に生まれて暮らしていることをラッキーだととらえている。本書を通して、私はこの国に生きることの面白みを、読者と分かちたい。

本書は、便宜上、いくつかのパートに分けてあるが、この分け方も全然体系的ではなく、「subtle」である。だから読者には、自分の興味の湧くところから読んでいただければ良いと思っている。

2018年初春、早速、たくさんの「曖昧なタブー」事件が起きている！

土屋　晴仁

and ambiguous things, and that is why they are so interesting and exciting. If everything is clear, and right and wrong are completely divided, **you could know about tomorrow even before the next day comes**, such a life wouldn't be worth living.

Japan is the champion of the "subtle" taboos, and that is why I feel lucky to be born and to have continued to live in this country. In this book, I'd like to share the joy of living in Japan with the readers.

The book is divided into several parts, but they are "subtle" divisions. So please just pick and choose the parts that look interesting for you.

It is now the springtime in 2018, and many incidents of "subtle taboos" are already happening!

Haruhito Tsuchiya

目次

Contents

Chapter 4. 消えるタブーと増えるタブー

Chapter 5. タブーと向き合うための５つのキーワード

CHAPTER
1

ガイジンが見つけた日本のタブー

Japanese taboos found by *gaijin*

2013年以来、日本に住み、ライターで経営コンサルタントでもあるカナダ国籍のグレッグ・ラムさんは（Mr. Greg Lam）、Webブログを YouTubeで発信している。最近の彼の記事で50万近くのアクセスがあったのは、「『ルール』が支配するニッポン（The Rules that Rule Japan）」というもの。彼が日本で見かけた光景の中から、日本らしいと思える「ルール」をユーモアたっぷりに紹介している。そのいくつかを元に、私なりの解説も加えてみたい。

Mr. Greg Lam, a Canadian writer and business consultant, has lived in Japan since 2013 and writes his blog on YouTube. His recent blog "The Rules that Rule Japan" was viewed nearly 500,000 times. He introduces "rules" that he thinks are very unique to Japan in an extremely humorous way. Based on some of his articles, I want to add my comments on those rules.

日本は「右側通行」なのか「左側通行」なのか？

日本は「**人は右、車は左**」の交通ルールがある。これは英国やオーストラリア、インド、シンガポールなど旧大英帝国の影響が強かった国でも共通である。人口比率にしたら世界の35%がこのルールに従っている。「Right is Right」(右側通行は正しい）とグレッグさん。

「しかし……」とグレッグさんは疑問を持つ。「道路は**右側通行**なのに、駅の構内などでは左側通行を指示している場所がたくさんある。これはなぜだ？」と。典型的なのが、エスカレーターで、人々は左に寄り、急ぐ人のために右側を空けるというとても**日本的な光景**だという。だが、彼は「いや、違う！　大阪は逆に右に寄っているではないか」と鋭く観察している。

そうなのだ。厳密にいうと京都駅の新幹線から**在来線や私鉄**の構内に入ると、この「左右逆転現象」が起きる。京都・大阪・奈良あたりの（つまり「近畿圏」の）エスカレーターでは、人々は右側に寄っている。ところがややこしいことに、もっと西に行って中国・四国・九州になると、また「左寄り」に戻るのだから、「関西圏」「西日本エリア」がそうなっているというのでもない。他にも色々な例を挙げることができるのだが、「近畿圏」は、どこか深いところに**“異国的”な遺伝子**が潜んでいるのかもしれない。

Right-hand or left-hand traffic in Japan?

In Japan, **cars drive on the left side of the road while pedestrians walk on the right**. This is the same in the U.K. and the countries where the former British Empire's influence was strong such as Australia, India, and Singapore. About 35% of the world population follows the same rule. Greg-san says, "Right is Right."

"But…" he wonders, "while **right is right** on the road, left is right in many places like at train stations. Why?" A typical example is, according to him, people ride on the left side of an escalator and leave the right side for the people in a hurry. This **looks like a very Japanese way**, but his keen observation points out that people ride on the right side of an escalator in Osaka.

He is right. To be more precise, when you get off bullet trains at Kyoto Station and change trains at the stations of **local or private lines**, you will see this "left and right reverse phenomenon." On escalators in Kyoto, Osaka, and Nara (located in Kinki area), people ride on the right side. But to make the phenomenon more complicated, people ride on the left side of an escalator in further west Japan, such as Chugoku, Shikoku, and Kyushu area. So, you can't simply divide this matter as broadly as Kansai or western Japan. I can point out various other examples of this kind about the "Kinki area." Deep inside this area, there may be some **"foreign" genes** residing.

神社と寺はどう違うのか？

グレッグさん一家は、日本の神社や寺にも出かける。神社と寺は「鳥居」や「墓地」の有無で見分けるという。神社には「鳥居」があり、寺には「墓地」があって、混在することはない。どちらも長い歴史の中で日本人の信仰と崇敬を集めてきた宗教施設である。

「しかし……」と彼はとまどう。**神社と寺とでは、拝礼の仕方が違う**からだ。神社では「**二礼二拍手一礼**」という拝礼のルールがあるが、寺では合掌するだけで、拍手はしてはいけないという。日本人の宗教的施設でありながら、どうしてこうも違う「ルール」なのか？

台東区浅草にある浅草寺は雷門などの写真で有名な**観光名所**の寺だが、その左（正面から見たら右隣り）には浅草神社がある。ここに来たガイジンは、絶対にとまどい、間違いを冒すだろう。「でも大丈夫。ガイジンだからと許されるよ」とグレッグさんは、「不思議で、違い過ぎるニッポン」にとまどう同僚たちを励ましている。

What is the difference between shrines and temples?

The Lams visit shrines and temples in Japan. They can tell the difference between shrines and temples by the existence of a "*torii*" or "cemetery." A shrine has a "*torii*" gate and a temple has a "cemetery," and they are not interchangeable. They are both religious facilities that have attracted Japanese religions and respect in the long history of Japan. But Greg-san gets confused because of **the different way respect is paid at shrines and temples**. At shrines, the ritual is "**bow twice, clap your hands twice, then bow once more**." But at temples, you are not supposed to clap your hands. Why are the rules so different?

Sensō-ji Temple in Asakusa, Taitō ward, is **one of the famous tourist spots**. Its Kaminari-mon is often featured in pictures. At the left side of the Sensō-ji is the Asakusa Shrine. If a *gaijin* visits this shrine, he or she would definitely be confused and makes the mistake of clapping hands there. "No worries. It won't be a big deal because you are *gaijin*," says Greg-san, and he encourages his fellow *gaijin* lost in the "deeply mysterious Japanese rituals."

実はこの作法は、日本人でも間違う。73歳になる私の叔母も、先日、死んだ夫の**法事**で盛大に「二拍手」してしまった。この作法はさらにややこしい。島根県の出雲大社や大分県の宇佐神宮などでは「二礼四拍手一礼」である。日本人でも、こんなことを知っている人は少ないだろうし、どうしてそうなっているのかまで知る人は、専門家だけだろう。

Even Japanese themselves make mistakes in this religious custom. Truth be told, my 73-year-old aunt "clapped her hands twice" without any hesitation at her late husband's **memorial service**. But wait; this custom can get more confusing. At the Izumo Taisha shrine in Shimane prefecture and the Usa Jingū shrine in Ōita Prefecture, the correct way of praying is: bow twice, clap the hands four times, then bow once more. Very few Japanese would know about this custom, and only a specialist would know the reason behind it.

喫煙者のための“聖域”まである

グレッグさんたち、洗練されたガイジンさんにとって“禁煙”は普通のことである。しかし、日本に来て驚くのは、飲食店などで「**分煙**」と称して「喫煙室」を設けていたり、駅や繁華街の一角に周囲に目隠しするように囲いを設けた「喫煙スペース」があることだ。グレッグさんは、これも**副流煙**を少なくして「他人に迷惑をかけないため」の配慮なのだろうと受け止めているが、喫煙者のための**“聖域”**まである光景は明らかに異様だ。

喫煙者が強く非難されるのは、副流煙よりも歩きながらの喫煙と**吸い殻の「ポイ捨て」**だ。危険でもあるし美観も損なう。

2002年、日本で最初に一番厳しい「歩行喫煙禁止ルール」を**条例**にしたのは、東京の千代田区である。警官や民間ボランティアが**違反者**を摘発して罰金2000円を徴収している。その千代田区が、「歩行喫煙禁止」を呼びかける際に使った、当初のキャッチフレーズは「マナーからルールへ」だった。その目的は、「歩きながら煙草を吸ったり、吸い殻を道路に捨てるのは常識的にマナー違反。でも、守ってくれないから、条例というルールにしましたよ」という周知のためだった。以来、15年以上経過して、摘発件数は年ごとに増減を繰り返している。では、効果がないのか、というとそうではないらしい。路上の吸い殻が多かった秋葉原などで**定点観測**を続けた結果、その数は確実に減少しているという。

“Sacred area” for smokers

For cultivated *gaijin* like Greg-san, “non-smoking” is an ordinary thing. So, when they come to Japan, they are surprised to see a “smoking room” in a restaurant claiming **separate areas for smokers and non-smokers**, or a “designated smoking space” surrounded by fences in the corners of train stations or busy streets. Greg-san thinks of it as a consideration to reduce **second-hand smoking** and “avoid bothering other people.” But this “**sacred area**” for smokers is abnormal for sure.

More than second-hand smoking, what smokers are blamed for the most is smoking while walking and **throwing away cigarette butts on the streets**. It is dangerous and damages the beautiful scenery as well.

In 2002, Chiyoda ward in Tokyo made the strictest **ordinance** “ban of smoking while walking.” When police officers or civilian volunteers find the **offenders** of this ordinance, they collect 2,000-yen fines. The original slogan that Chiyoda ward used for the “ban of smoking while walking” was “From manners to rules.” The purpose of the slogan was to let the citizens know that “Smoking while walking and throwing away the cigarette butts on the roads are bad manners. But as manners don’t have the power to stop the bad behavior, we set a rule (ordinance).” It has been more than 15 years since this ordinance was created, but the number

そこで千代田区は考え直した。条例を厳しくして違反者を減らすよりも、やはり人々の常識や**公共意識**、マナーを守る気持ちに訴えるべきだと。そこで5年後の2007年にキャッチフレーズを変更した。「マナーからルールへ。そしてマナーへ」と。この言葉を看板などに盛り込んで、JR飯田橋駅出口など千代田区内にたくさん掲示するようになった。

でも「マナー」と「ルール」をループするようなこのキャッチフレーズは、正直言ってわかりにくい。キャッチ・コピーとしては落第だ。だが、これまでの経緯や行政の思い入れを理解すれば、このような表現になった理由もうなずける。

参考までに書くと、日本の喫煙率は1966年の83.7%（成人男性）をピークに減少を続けており、現在は19.3%とほぼOECD加盟国の平均値になった。グレッグさんの母国カナダは14.9%、米国は11.4%。日本は、禁煙トレンドの**過渡期**にあるようだ。

of the exposures fluctuates depending on the year. Does it mean this ordinance is not effective? According to the continuing **fixed-point observations** in Akihabara and other places, where a lot of cigarette butts had been seen on the roads, the number of thrown-away cigarettes is said to be decreasing steadily.

Then, Chiyoda ward changed its mind. It decided to appeal to people's common sense, **sense of community**, and emotions to keep good manners, rather than forcing strict ordinance to reduce the number of offenders. So, in 2007, Chiyoda ward changed the slogan to "From manners to rules, and back to manners." It put this slogan on billboards and put them at the exits of JR Iidabashi Station and many other places in the ward.

To be honest, this slogan, which loops between manners and rules, is hard to understand, and an awful one. But if you understand the history behind it and what the administration was hoping to, the expression in the slogan could be understandable to some extent.

For your information, the smoking rate in Japan in 1966 was as high as 83.7% (adult male), and it has been decreasing since then. Currently, it is 19.3%, which is about average in OECD member states. In Canada, Greg-san's homeland, the smoking rate is 14.9%, and in the U.S., 11.4%. It looks like Japan is in the **transition period** from a smoking to a non-smoking trend.

「ルール」がなさ過ぎる建物

グレッグさんは、日本の「ルール」が多すぎることだけを指摘しているのではない。逆に**建築規制**などには「ルールがなさ過ぎではないか」と疑問を投げかける。オフィスビルの傍に神社があったり、猫の額ほどの小さな面積に細長いビル（通称「ペンシルビル」）が建っていたりするからだ。これが海外なら、**地区ごとのイメージを損なう建築計画**に対しては、住民が敏感に反応して反対運動を起こしたりするのに、日本ではそういうことが少ないという。

しかし、グレッグさんの指摘には少し誤解がある。近年、日本でも各自治体が、**景観に配慮**した街づくりを進めるようになってきた。東京・新宿区の場合、学者や町内会役員そして民間委員など10数名によって「景観まちづくり審議会」というものが設置され、大規模な建築計画の場合、この審議会に意見を諮らねばならない。委員たちから、ビルのデザインなどについて「高すぎる」とか、「歩道側の樹木を増やして」、「防犯上、植え込みが**死角**にならないか」などの意見が出されたら、施主や建築会社は計画を見直し、改善結果を報告することになっている。（不肖、私もその委員の**はしくれ**であるが……）

No rules for buildings

Greg-san points out there are too many rules in Japan, but he also questions the lack of rules of the **building regulations**. There are cases where a shrine exists right next to an office building, or a very thin and tall building (so-called "pencil building") is built on an extremely small piece of land. If this were the case in other countries, Greg-san continues, residents would oppose a **building plan that could damage the image of the area**, but such movement is rare in Japan.

But let me point out that Greg-san misunderstands Japan's situation a little. Recently, each local government has started to proceed with city development with **consideration for the scenery**. In Shinjuku ward in Tokyo, for example, the "Scenic city development committee" was established by about ten members including scholars, the officers of the neighborhood associations, and private sector members, and a large development plan has to be discussed at this committee. The members of the committee will present opinions about the building plan such as the height, the number of trees on the pedestrian side street, and the security concern of a possible **dead zone** created by the vegetation. Then, the client and the construction company must review the plan and submit the improved plan to the committee. (Just for your information, I am

京都などは建物の高さ制限や看板類の配色などに厳しい。あのマクドナルドやセブンイレブンも市内では、地味な、周囲に溶け込んだ看板にしている。遅すぎの感はあるが、日本ももう少し秩序のある街並みにしようとして動いてはいるのだ。

なおグレッグさんは、このゴチャゴチャした町並みをひどいと言っているわけではない。規制の少なかった時代にできたアナーキーな建物たちが作る風景や、路地裏などに**日本独自の風情**もあるではないか、と指摘しているのである。

one of the members of this committee.)

Kyoto has strict building restrictions for building heights or color selections of billboards. Even McDonald's and Seven-Eleven have subdued signs matching the neighborhood environment. It was a slow start, but Japan is now trying to make more orderly townscapes than before.

Just to make sure, Greg-san is not criticizing Japan's chaotic townscapes. Rather, he points out that he can see the **unique Japanese touch** in the anarchy buildings from the era when there were few restrictions, or in the narrow back streets.

結論、「日本的『ルール』を守って住めば快適だ」

グレッグさんのブログは、旅行やビジネスで来日するガイジン仲間に向けて書かれている。他にもたくさんの記事をアップしていてそれぞれに面白いが、やはり20万以上のアクセスがある最近の記事に、「日本でやってはならない12のこと（12 Things NOT to do in Japan）」というのがある。たとえば、「歩きながらの飲食はだめ」、「箸の使い方を間違うな」、「“チップ”を置くな」、「公共交通機関での携帯通話はだめ」、「名刺の使い方を間違うな」、「人前で鼻をかむな」、「室内では靴を脱げ」……など身近な、そして**彼なりの体験を踏まえた**「文化的エチケット」を12ほど挙げている。なんだか、ここまでナーバスにならなくても良いのではないか？　と思える。よほどマジメな人なのだろう。いや、彼自身も、これらのエチケットの羅列を「少しナーバスかも」と感じたらしく、その12番目のエチケットは、「キリストたるな！」とある。日本語で言えば「聖人君子であることはない」と言うのである。

暮らしてきた文化的背景が違うのだから、色んな失敗があって当然だ。日本では、主張や自己表現が実に「subtle（曖昧）で、時として芸術的である」、「集団としての思考、**横並びの行動**が尊重される文化だ」と指摘する。だから、前述したブログでも、最後の画面にこんなオチをつけた。「赤信号、みんなで渡れば怖くない（Red light aren't scary when you're crossing together）」。これは映画監督として有名になった北野武が、コメディアン時代（芸名：

Conclusion: Obey the rules and you can live comfortably in Japan

Greg-san's blog is written for *gaijin* tourists and business persons. He has uploaded many other interesting articles, but the recent one titled "12 Things NOT to do in Japan," which has had more than 200,000 viewings, is excellent. He lists "cultural etiquettes" in everyday life **based on his experiences** as follows: DON'T eat & drink while walking; DON'T do various things with chopsticks; DON'T tip; DON'T use your phone on public transport; DON'T underestimate the importance of business cards; DON'T blow your nose in public; DON'T forget to take off your shoes, etc. In my opinion, he doesn't have to be that nervous, but then, he must be a very serious person. He must have felt that the list of these etiquettes is "a bit too nervous" and put the 12th etiquette as "DON'T CHRIST. DON'T worry about not knowing Japanese etiquette."

It is natural to make mistakes in foreign countries because your cultural background is different. He points out that the self-appealing and self-expression in Japan are "subtle and sometimes artistic," and "it is a culture where people think as a group and **act as the others do**." So, he ended his blog saying, "Red lights aren't scary when you're crossing together." It is a very popular joke by Takeshi Kitano, a famous movie

ビートたけし）に流行させたギャグ（ジョーク）である。たしかに、「停止」を意味する交差点の赤信号も、全員が無視してしまえば車が止まらざるを得ない。つまりルールが無力化する。だが、こんな言葉が、ギャグとして通用するのは、日本社会だからではないか。

親日家で知的で繊細なグレッグさんが、一連のWebブログで伝えたかったことは、「ガイジンの同僚諸君、日本はたしかにstrange and differentな『ルール』がたくさんあるけど、『他人に迷惑をかけないように』という“**黄金律**”があることと、その場の『**空気を読む**』ことの大切さを知っておけば、とても快適に暮らせる国だよ。Easy-peasy（とっても簡単なこと）さ」ということのようだ。ガイジンだけでなく、日本人が観てもなかなか面白い記事が多いので、一度見ることをおすすめする。
（URLはhttp://www.lifewhereimfrom.com/）

director when he was a comedian named Beat Takeshi. Surely, if everybody ignores the red light meaning "do not cross" at the crossroad, cars would have to stop. The rule becomes powerless. But I think that only in Japan could such a joke pass as a gag.

What Greg-san, who is intellectual, sensitive, and loves Japan, wanted to say in the series of his blog was this: "My fellow *gaijin*, I know there are many strange and different 'rules' in Japan. But if you follow the **Golden Rule** of 'Don't trouble the others' and know the importance of **'read the air' of your surroundings**, it is a comfortable country to live in. It's easy-peasy." His blog is highly recommended not only to *gaijin* but Japanese as well.
(URL: http://www.lifewhereimfrom.com/)

CHAPTER 2

昨今の気になる事件とタブー

The incidents surrounding taboos happened recently

人類はサルより賢くて、善良で、進化し続けている生き物か？　毎日、世界中のどこかで起きている事件や事故を見る限り答えは「No!」だ。その事件や事故にしても、特定の集団の中で守られてきたルールを破ったり、守られてきた「タブー」を冒すものがある。それも一向に減らない。ためしに、あるひと月の期間（2017年11月）だけに限って、いくつかの**事例**を見てみよう。これらは、決して、特別（例外的）なものではない。これからも起きる。まず、世界で起きたことから……。

- インドネシア・ジャカルタでは、2015年にできた**蝋人形館**で展示していたヒットラーの像を撤去した。米国のユダヤ人人権団体「サイモン・ウィーゼンタール・センター（Simon Wiesenthal Center）」などの批判を受けたからだ。**ヒットラーやナチズム礼賛**へのタブー、それを批判する世論は根強い。

- サッカー韓国代表とコロンビア代表の強化試合で、コロンビアの選手が、韓国の選手に対して、両手で**目をつり上げるポーズ**を取り、人種差別的行為にあたると批判を浴びて謝罪した。また、ほぼひと月前には、野球のメジャーリーグのワールドシリーズで、アストロズの内野手が、ドジャースの日本人投手ダルビッシュ有に対して同様の行為をして、後に謝罪している。**人種的偏見**を露わにすることも「タブー」である。

Is a human being wiser and better than a monkey? Are we the creatures that keep on developing? When I see accidents and incidents happening all over the world every day, my answers to those questions are "No!" Some of the incidents or accidents include the cases where the rules and taboos were broken that had been kept within a certain group. The number of such cases has not decreased at all. Let's take a look at the real **cases** that happened within a month (November 2017). These are not exceptional, and similar incidents would occur for sure. First, on the world front:

- In Jakarta, Indonesia, Hitler's figure was removed from a **wax house** opened in 2015 due to the criticism by a Jewish human rights group (Simon Wiesenthal Center) in the U.S. **Praising Hitler and Nazism** is a taboo backed by strong public opinion.

- At the warm-up soccer matches between Korean and Columbian representative teams, a Columbian athlete made a **slant-eyed gesture**, which was criticized as a racist one. He apologized for his action. Also, one month earlier than this incident, an infielder of Astros made the same gesture to Yu Darvish, a Japanese pitcher of Dodgers, at the major league world series, and he later apologized for his rudeness. To reveal one's **racial discrimination** is one of the taboos.

● 数々のオスカーも受賞したハリウッドの**大物映画プロデューサー**が、過去30年近くにわたって、多くの女優などにセクハラを行っていたことが、女優の告発によって明らかにされた。プロデューサーは、弟と共同設立した会社から解雇。事実上、ハリウッドを追放された。特権的な立場を利用したセクハラ事件は、「パンドラの箱」を空けたかのように、その後も、有名監督や俳優だけでなく各界VIPに対しても類似の告発が続いている。米国キニピアック大学(Quinnipiac University)の世論調査では、女性有権者の約60%が、「セクハラを経験したことがある」と答えた。これは「#METOO(私も被害者)」というSNS内のキャンペーンになって未だに“炎上”を続けている。

……これらは日々起きている事件の**ほんのかけら**に過ぎない。ナチス・タブー、人種・女性・障害者への差別。頻発するこれらの事件が、人々の心のどこかを刺激するのはなぜだろう？　「タブー」と差別は、どこかで**密接に関係している**ことが感じられる。……いや、深堀りするのは後回しにしよう。同時期に起きていた日本の“事件”を見てからにしよう。

- A Hollywood's **big shot movie producer**, who had received several Oscars, was sued by many actresses for sexual harassment for nearly 30 years. He was fired by the company that he had started with his brother, and in fact, expelled from Hollywood. Many lawsuits are following for similar sexual harassment by powerful people including famous movie directors, actors, and VIPs of various industries. It is almost like opening Pandora's Box. According to a poll conducted by Quinnipiac University in the U.S., about 60% of women voters replied that they had experienced sexual harassments. This has become the "#METOO" campaign on SNS and is still very active.

These are **just a few examples** of the incidents that are happening every day; the taboo against Nazis, and discriminations against race, women, and disabled people. Why do these incidents stimulate somewhere in our hearts? Are taboos and discriminations **closely related** to each other? Before answering these questions, I'd like you to read about the following incident that was happening around the same time in Japan.

21世紀によみがえった「村八分」事件

大分県北部のわずか14世帯が住む小さな集落で「**村八分**」事件が起きた。事件は、大分県弁護士会がこの集落の自治会に対して、「ある住民男性（68歳）に『村八分』のような扱いをしている。他の住民と平等に扱うように」という**人権侵害の是正勧告**したことから表面化した。この男性は、2009年に母親の介護と就農のために**自分のふるさとであるこの集落にUターン**した。しかし農地開拓の補助金の配分を受けられないなどの差別を受け、2013年には行事連絡や市報の配布先からも除外され、集落の構成員から外された。

今回の事件に対して、自治会側はこの男性が住民票を移していないとか、自治会への入会手続きをしないなどの理由をあげて「村八分」の事実はないと反論している。しかし大分県弁護士会では、過去にも県内の別の集落で類似の事件が起きていたことから、今回は**是正勧告という措置に踏み切った**という。だが、それ以降目立った進展はないままだ。

Social ostracism revived in the 21st century

Ostracism happened in a small village with only 14 households in the northern part of Ōita Prefecture. This incident has surfaced after the **citation of violation for human rights** by the Ōita Bar Association against the residents' association of this village. The content of the citation was that a 68-year-old male resident of this village was ostracized and he should be treated equally as other villagers. The man **came back to his home village** in 2009 to care for his mother and start farming. He, however, was discriminated against and could not receive the allocation of subsidies for the farm land reclamation. In 2013, he was taken off the list of event news or the city newsletter delivery and finally expelled from the members of the community.

The residents' association argues against the allegation. It explained its action was based on the fact that the man had not moved his resident's card to the village, and he had not completed the sign-up procedures for the residents' association yet. A similar incident had happened at another village in the same prefecture in the past. So, the Ōita Bar Association **decided to recommend corrective action** this time. No progress has been made since then.

日本の「村八分」というのは、村落（村社会）の中で、掟や秩序を破った者に対して課される**制裁行為**であった。地域の生活における成人式、結婚式、出産、病気の世話、新改築の手伝い、水害時の世話、年忌法要、旅行など10の共同行為のうち、放置すると他の人間に迷惑のかかる葬式の世話と消火活動の2つだけを除いて、つまり80%の交流を絶つ**共同絶交というか集団的ないじめ**である。だが、都会に住む多くの人は、現代日本には「村八分」など存在しないと思っていたから、この事件に何世紀も昔に引き戻される気分がしただろう。

しかし「村八分」事件は、これからも各地で起きる可能性はある。ゴミの収集、**里山**の共同利用、農業用水路の掃除、**祭礼**の運営など、小さな村落の住民たちが長年にわたってルールを作り、守ってきた共同体の暮らしが、高齢化や人口流出などで維持できなくなってきていることが背景にある。ルールを知らない新参者や、共同体のルールより自分の利害を優先する一部の人たちが「問題」を起こしてしまう。これまで集落をまとめてきた**長老**たちが不在になれば、その亀裂は深刻化するが、自治を尊重する立場の行政や警察には**仲介**しにくい案件にな

Mura-Hachibu in Japan was a **way to punish** people who broke law and order in village society. There are ten community events such as adulthood, wedding, birth, illness, building or renovating a house, flooding, funeral, travel, and so forth. All the members of the community ignore and do not help the punished people except for the occasions of funeral and fire because of the danger to the others. It meant stopping 80% of communication with the punished and **mass breach or bullying**. Most of the city people, who think that ostracism no longer exists in modern day Japan, must have a hard time believing that this is happening now and not many centuries ago.

The ostracism could happen in various places even now. In small villages, residents have been making their rules and kept their lives as a community for a long time in such situations as garbage collections, shared uses of the **nearby mountains**, cleaning of the irrigation canals, and operation of **festivals**. But those things are becoming difficult due to the aged society and the population outflow. Newcomers who don't know the rules, or a small number of people who put their interests first and ignore the rules of the community, will cause problems. **Senior members** of the villages have been kept the communities together. When they are gone, it would be difficult for the government or the police to **intervene** in the communities because the villages

る。17世紀の「タブー」が21世紀に蘇る可能性は大いにある。

respect the autonomy. There is a strong possibility that the 17th century's taboo might be coming back in the 21st century.

有名人スキャンダル報道にも自主規制

不倫、薬物、暴力、汚職など、政界や芸能界などの有名人が引き起こすスキャンダルは相変わらず多いが、その報道での扱われ方に不思議な濃淡がある。

たとえば、ある有名な競馬騎手が、若い女性タレントと不倫したと報道され、それなりに**世間を騒がせた**。しかし、他の類似の事件では、公式会見を開いて謝罪したり、職を辞したりするところまで"炎上"して騒ぎが大きくなることも多いのに、彼の場合は、"ボヤ"程度ですまされた。

"事情をよく知るTV局のプロデューサー"という人が非公式に発言した話を追うと、「彼（騎手）の**女グセの悪さ**は昔から有名だ。しかし競馬界は、マスコミの大スポンサーであり、彼はスター選手。スポンサーが圧力をかけなくても、マスコミが**自主規制**して、事件を後追いしないことは、最初から分かっていた」というのである。

この手の話に必ず登場する正体不明の"**業界通**"の証言など、どこまで真相を伝えるものかは怪しい。しかし、ありえない話でないだろう。業界のタブー、マスコミのタブーというものは確実に存在するようだ。中には、そうしたタブーを冒し、プレッシャーを受けながらも調査と報道を続けた結果、人々の意識を啓発したり社会悪を摘

Self-restriction of reporting about the scandals of the rich and famous

Adultery, drug, corruption ... there are many scandals by famous people such as politicians and celebrities. Strangely, however, the media coverage varies depending on each case.

For example, a famous horse jockey had an affair with a young female TV personality, and it hardly **made a flutter**. In other similar cases, usually the news would become big headlines, and people who are involved usually have press conferences to apologize or resign from the positions. But in his case, it didn't reach that point.

A TV producer, who knows the background of this matter in detail, has stated "It has been well known that he (the jockey) is a **womanizer**. But the horse racing industry is a big media sponsor and he is a star jockey. We knew from the beginning that the media would exercise **self-restraint** and wouldn't pursue this incident seriously."

A "**well-informed person in the industry**" always appears when this kind of incident happens, but we are not sure if his or her comment is close to the truth. But it could be true. It looks like industry and media taboos surely exist. There are cases that some reporters bravely ignore the taboos, and continue the research,

発したりして、意義のある結果が出せる場合もある。しかし、これが不倫のような問題となると、どう告発しようが、世間の**「野次馬」的好奇心**を満たせばそれ以上先に進みにくい。ましてやカネにならないのなら、煽り立てる次の標的（“火元”）探しに走るのが、マスコミの本能だ。

and report despite the pressure. As a result, they could change people's thinking or reveal social ills. When it comes to adultery, the media give the information that satisfies people's **curiosities**, and usually will not go further than that. The media's instinct is to move on to the next target if the current one is not profitable.

形骸化したコンプライアンスと記者会見

このひと月で目立ったのは、日本を代表する大手製造業の企業による品質管理に関する不祥事だった。日産、SUBARUの無資格検査、さらに神戸製鋼や三菱マテリアル、東レ、三菱アルミの**品質データ改ざん**……。

企業コンプライアンス（regulatory compliance）によって、**法律や内規などを順守**し、またISOなどの国際的な品質規格に従って、厳正な企業統治（corporate governance）ができていると思われてきたビッグ企業の相次ぐ不祥事の発覚である。実態が明るみになって、その**杜撰な管理体制**が知られるにつれて、「モノ作り大国・ニッポン」の将来を心配する声が高まってきたのも無理はない。でも、本書はそのことを話題にするものではない。連日の報道を見ながら呆れたのは、記者会見でのワンパターンぶりだった。

こうした事件の場合、記者会見では、まず関係部署の役員が、「（このような事件は）あってはならないこと。管理職を含め、しっかりと従業員教育をしていく」と表明する。そして引き連れている他のメンバーと共に立ち上がり、数十秒間深々と「お詫び」のお辞儀をするのが、一つの**カ**

A mere shell of compliance and a press conference

In the past month, the big news was the incidents regarding the quality controls by Japan's big companies: the quality checks by non-certified technicians of Nissan and Subaru, the **quality data falsification** by Kobe Steel, Mitsubishi Materials, Toray and Mitsubishi Aluminum.

We have been assured that those big firms **obey the laws and internal regulations** based on the regulatory compliances, and they conduct strict corporate governance according to the international quality control regulations such as ISO. As their realities and **poor control systems** have become apparent, it is understandable that people have started to worry about the future of Japan as "the big industrial power." But that is not what I want to write about in this book. What I want to write about is that I was appalled by the attitude of the executives of those companies; they all acted in the same way at the press conferences.

The following is the **pattern** at a press conference: first, the executives of the related departments would say, "This (the incident) shouldn't have happened. From now on, we will re-educate our employees including the management staff." Then, they all stand up with

タチになってしまった。もう少し深い反省をする場合は、まず上級役員の責任と懲罰を明らかにし、「**社外の有識者による調査委員会**を設けて、事件の真相解明と再発防止策を立てて実行します」と表明する。だがその経過や結果（効果）についてまで、継続的に真摯に公開するケースはごくわずかだ。

過去には、記者会見で失言したばかりに世間の批判を増幅させたケースもたくさんあった。その教訓からこういうパターンが"完成"したのだろうが、まるで謝意が感じられない。どうやら企業が掲げるコンプライアンスの精神までも**形骸化**してしまっているようだ。ルールを厳格化し、細部まで規制することによって、かえって疲弊しているのかもしれない。本当に深刻なのはこちらの問題だと思うが……。

思い出すのは、ほぼ20年前、1997年11月の、**山一證券の廃業**である。不正会計とバブル崩壊で**経営破たんした**大手証券会社が、自主的に廃業することを公表したのだが、会見した野澤正平社長は、投資家と社員たちにお詫びの言葉を涙ながらに伝えた。廃業という選択は最悪のも

another member who came along and deeply bow for twenty to thirty seconds to express their remorse. To express deeper remorse, they first make clear the responsibility and punishment of the executives related to the incident, and say, "We will set up an **investigation committee consisted of experts outside the company** to find out the truth and get advice on the prevention of such an incident. And we will follow the advised actions." But it is very rare that they will continue to report sincerely and continuously about the status and the result (effectiveness) of the actions taken.

In the past, there were many cases where the speeches at press conferences provoked further criticism by the public. Those past cases could be the cause of the creation of this "pattern," but it is hard to feel their sincerity in there. It looks like the spirit of compliance has merely **turned into a formality**. Stricter rules and detailed regulations might have made the compliance too difficult to follow. This, in my opinion, is a more serious problem than the pattern expressed at a press conference.

I remember when **Yamaichi Securities went out of business** around 20 years ago, in November 1997. This big security company **went bankrupt** because of the accounting fraud and collapse of the bubble economy. When it announced its voluntary business closure,

のだったが、経営トップたるものの姿勢としては立派だった。少なくとも、表面だけでなく心のこもったものだった。今、そんな経営者はほとんどいない。

Shohei Nozawa, president of the company, expressed his apologies, with tears in his eyes, to the investors and employees at the press conference. The bankruptcy was the worst choice, but Nozawa's attitude as top management was impressive because he spoke from his heart. This level of sincerity from managers is not often seen these days.

反捕鯨グループの実力行使

2017年10月下旬、和歌山・白浜のレジャー施設「アドベンチャーワールド」で、イルカショーが行われていたプールにウエットスーツ姿のオランダ人とベルギー人の男女２人が飛び込んだ。そしてイルカ漁に抗議するプラカードを水中で高々と掲げてショーを妨害した。別の男はそれを撮影。彼らの属する**動物愛護団体**はインターネット上で犯行予告もしていた。３人は**威力業務妨害容疑**で県警に逮捕されたが、反省の様子はなく、まるで英雄気取りだった。

過去にも、反捕鯨団体「シー・シェパード」による日本の調査捕鯨への妨害がたくさんあった。日本人は昔から鯨類を**貴重なたんぱく源**として食してきたが、食文化が違う世界の人々は、「友好的で知性ある動物を食べるなんて」と批判してきた。当然ながら日本人たちには、この批判は受け入れがたい。世界にはさまざまな民族が、固有の環境と歴史の中で固有の食文化を育んできたと考えるのが、理性的な思考に思えるのに、なぜ鯨類に関してかくも**感情的**になるのか？

Use of force by the anti-whaling group

This incident happened in late October a Dutch and a Belgian wearing wet suits jumped into a pool where a dolphin show was taken place at Adventure World, a leisure facility in Shirahama, Wakayama prefecture. They interrupted the show by hoisting up placards to protest dolphin fishing. Another man was shooting the scene. The **animal protection group** they belong to had announced this protesting action in advance on the Internet. Those three people were arrested on **allegations of forcible obstruction of business** by the Wakayama Prefecture Police, but they showed no remorse and acted as if they were heroes.

In the past, Japan's whaling research has often been blocked by the Sea Shepherd Conservation Society, an anti-whaling group. The Japanese have been eating whales as a **source of precious protein**. But other countries with a different food culture have been criticizing Japan, claiming that it is unimaginable to eat such a friendly and intelligent animal. That kind of criticism is not acceptable for Japanese people, of course. It would be rational to think that various ethnic groups have unique food cultures based on their environment and histories. But why do people get so **emotional** about whales?

歴史的事実として、19世紀の米国は、鯨から**燃料用油脂**分を採るだけのために乱獲し、東アジアまで遠征してきた。また日本の調査捕鯨では、現在の資源量に悪影響を与えないような捕獲頭数を科学的手法により算出し、その頭数の範囲内で捕獲。1頭1頭のクジラから、それぞれ100項目以上の科学データが収集されている。その分析結果は、毎年国際捕鯨委員会（IWC）科学委員会に報告されて高い評価を得ている。調査後の鯨肉が市販されるのは、**国際捕鯨取締条約**にある規定「捕獲したクジラは可能な限り加工して利用しなければならない」にもとづくものだ。

反捕鯨グループの執拗な妨害活動を見ていると、そのバックで何かしら国際的な“**影の力**”が働いているのかもしれないと思える。「シー・シェパード」が2017年夏になって急に活動停止を発表したのも疑いを深める。彼らは、感情でも信念でもない“何かの力”で活動してきたのではないか、と。しかし、まだその正体は明らかにならない。彼らを調査報道する国際的なネットワークができていないからだ。今のところ“**影の力**”を語るのはタブーだ。

In fact, historically, the U.S. caught a lot of whales just to get their **oil for fuel**, and they hunted them as far as East Asia in the 19th century. Also, Japan's whaling research has been conducted in a way to ensure that it doesn't cause detrimental influences on the current numbers of whales based on a scientific calculation, and it collects more than 100 items of scientific data per one whale. Its analyzed data has been reported to the Scientific Committee of the International Whaling Commission (IWC) and is receiving a positive reputation. After the research, the whale meat has been sold to the market, based on the **Article of the International Convention for the Regulation of Whaling** which states, "Any whales taken under these special permits shall so far as practicable be processed..."

There might be some international **mastermind** pulling strings behind the persistent obstructive activities by the anti-whaling group. If we think this way, it makes sense that the Sea Shepherd stopped its activities abruptly in the summer of 2017; it might have been acting backed by "some kind of power" rather than based on its feeling or belief. The face of that power, however, hasn't been revealed because there are no international networks to investigate and report on it. For now, it is taboo to talk about this "**power behind the scenes**."

「可愛がり」過ぎた横綱の引退騒動

大相撲の横綱でモンゴル出身の日馬富士が、若い力士を殴ったことの責任を取って引退することになった。事件の真相がすべて明らかになったわけではないが、鳥取市に**巡業中**のある夜、**モンゴル出身力士同士の懇親会**で、同席した若手力士の不作法さに腹を立てた日馬富士が、カラオケのマイクや素手で殴り、相当の傷を負わせたと報じられた。

日馬富士は引退表明の会見で、「弟弟子が礼儀と礼節がなっていなかった時にそれを正し、直して教えてあげるのが**先輩**の義務だと思っています。弟弟子を思って叱ったことが彼を傷つけ、大変世間を騒がせて迷惑をかけることになってしまいました。**行き過ぎた**ことになりました。彼のためになる、僕が正しいことをしているという思いが強すぎた」と反省している。また「翌日にその力士と握手して和解したと思っていた」と語った。

彼の人となりを知る人は、「ふだん**酒が原因で暴力をふるうような人**ではない」とかばうし、彼は相撲の合間に「モンゴルの経済や教育を研究したい」と法政大学の大学院にも通っており、恩師も「非常にまじめで、知的好奇心がとても強い人だった」と証言する。将来は**親方として自**

The retirement of a *yokozuna* (grand champion of sumo) after "too much care" for his subordinate

Harumafuji, a Mongolian **grand champion of sumo**, announced his retirement after taking responsibility for hitting a younger sumo wrestler. Not all the facts of the case are clear yet, but it had been reported that Harumafuji got angry for the bad manners of the young sumo wrestler, and hit him with karaoke mike or his hands and injured him at a **Mongolian sumo wrestler gathering** one night **during the tour** in Tottori city.

At a press conference, Harumafuji said regretfully, "I think that it is the duty of the **upper level person** to point out and teach younger wrestlers when their manners are not proper. I scolded and disciplined my younger pupil for his sake, but it hurt him as a result, and it caused a lot of trouble. I think it **went too far**. I thought I was doing it for him, and I was doing the right thing." He also said, "As I shook hands with him the next day, I thought that we were all right."

A person who knows Harumafuji well defends him saying, "He is not the type of **person who becomes violent after drinking sake**." The *yokozuna* attends a post-graduation course at the Hosei University between the sumo tournaments to study the economy

分の部屋を持つ希望も持っていたというが、27歳でその夢は絶たれた。

相撲界では、「**可愛がり**」と称して、先輩力士が後輩を手荒く「**しごく**」ことが習慣になっていた。それが時に行き過ぎて**死傷事件**を起こしたこともあった。今回もその一つと見られるが、白鵬以下モンゴル出身者が上位を占めているために、悔しさの混じった厳しい眼で見られる現状もある。また、事件が大きく報道され、終息に時間がかかった背景には**相撲協会内部の対立**もあるという。彼のマジメな性格に複雑な力学が働いた引退騒動だった。

and education system in Mongolia. "He is very diligent and has a strong intellectual curiosity," commented his former teacher. It is said that Harumafuji was hoping to **become a stable master and have his own stable** in the future, but his dream became impossible at the age of twenty-seven.

In Sumo world, "**hazing**" lower ranked wrestlers has been customarily done by upper ranked wrestlers, and it is called "**pampering**." Sometimes it goes too far, and there have been **incidents of assault**. The incident on this occasion might be one of those cases. Currently, most of the upper titles of sumo are held by Mongolian wrestlers with the top being Hakuhō. Harumafuji's action could have been treated more severe than normal because of the bitter feelings toward the strong Mongolian wrestlers in general. Some say the reason why this incident was reported widely and took a long time for closure was the **confrontation inside the Japan Sumo Association**. Harumafuji's retirement was not simply based on his serious character, but also many other factors existed behind it.

「新嘗祭」の秘儀と天皇の生前退位

11月23日は、日本では「勤労感謝の日」という祝日になっているが、戦前には「新嘗祭（にいなめさい）」と呼ばれ、収穫の実りを祖先と天地に感謝する日とされたが、ルーツは7世紀から**宮中**に伝わる「天皇が行う儀式」に由来する。その概略を紹介しよう。

23日の夕方と深夜の2度、天皇は重い白絹の衣装をまとい、「神嘉殿」に入って**米と粟の新穀、新酒などを神前に供える儀式**を行う。2人の「采女（うねめ）」だけが手伝い、かすかな燈明の下、暖房もない状態で伝統の所作を行う。のべ4時間にも及ぶ儀式と伝えられるが、詳しいところは分かっていない。

体力的にあまりに過酷なので、昭和天皇は63歳で自分が行うことをやめているし、今の天皇も77歳からは時間を短縮したり、儀式の一部を省略することになった。しかし、儀式を代行する**侍従**らから終了の報告を受けるまでは就寝されずにいるという。

前の昭和天皇（1901 − 1989）もまじめな方だったが、現

The secret ceremony of the *Niiname-sai* festival and Emperor Akihito's abdication

November 23 is "Labor Thanksgiving Day" holiday in Japan. Before the war, it was called *Niiname-sai* festival, and it was the day to thank the ancestors and nature for the good harvest. Originally it was a "ceremony done by the emperor" at the **imperial court** in the 7th century. Here is the outline of this ceremony:

Once in the evening and another in the middle of the night on 23rd, the emperor wearing a heavy white silk costume goes into Shinka-den Hall, and conducts an **offering ceremony of a new crop of rice and millet, and fresh sake to the deities**. With only the assistance of two ***uneme* court ladies**, he performs the traditional gestures under the dim votive light in a cold place without any heaters. It is said that this ceremony takes in total four hours, but its details are unknown.

As it was so difficult, Emperor Showa stopped doing it by himself when he was sixty-three, and Emperor Akihito made it shorter or omitted part of the ceremony at the age of seventy-seven. But it is said that he doesn't sleep until he gets the completion report from the **chamberlains** who performed the ceremony for him.

Emperor Showa (1901–1989) was a conscientious

在の天皇（1933年生まれ）もまじめで誠実なお人柄である。心臓疾患の大病も経験したのに、美智子皇后とともに公式行事を**視察や慰問**、交流に国内外各地に出向かれる。その過密とも思える日程は、若い人でも疲れそうだ。

日本では天皇は亡くなるまでその地位に留まることが慣習として続いてきた。しかし公務をこなすのは高齢の現天皇には厳しすぎる。そこで生前に退位できる**特例法**が2017年6月に成立し、11月になって政府は退位の時期を2019年の4月末とした。**生前退位**は200年ぶりのことだという。

ところで、この「新嘗祭」をもっと大がかりにしたものが、新天皇の**即位**時に行われる「大嘗祭」である。この儀式もほんの一部しか公開されない。2019年春の新天皇即位の際でも公開されないはずだ。日本のマスコミは、宮内庁の“秘密主義”を皇室の紋章である「菊花紋」になぞらえて「**菊のカーテン**」と呼ぶが、そのカーテンがすべて開けられる日は、21世紀が終わっても来ないだろう。

person, and Emperor Akihito (born in 1933) is a sincere person as well. Despite having suffered from severe heart disease, he, along with Empress Michiko, travels all over Japan for official functions, **pays visits to console people, and for mingling with people**. Their schedule is very tight, and it would be hard even for a young person.

In Japan, it has been a custom that the emperor remains in the position until he dies. However, as it is becoming too hard for Emperor Akihito at his great age, a **special exemption law** was created in June 2017. In November of that year, the Japanese government announced the timing of the Emperor's retirement as the end of April 2019. The previous case of an **emperor's abdication** was 200 years ago.

The larger scale of *Niiname-sai* festival is *Daijō-sai* festival which takes place at the time of the new emperor's **enthronement**. Only part of this ceremony is open to the public. When new emperor assumes the throne, *Daijō-sai* festival will not be shown to the public. Japanese mass media calls the Imperial Household Agency's secrecy "**chrysanthemum curtain**" comparing it to the Imperial crest of the chrysanthemum. The agency's curtain would not be open all the way even after the 21st century.

以上のニュースは、2017年11月前後に起きた事件の一部である。日本人の多くは気づいていないかもしれないが、**歴史と文化が絡んだ非常に日本的な事件**である。外国人には、その背景をかなり説明しないと理解されない側面がある。21世紀になって、ライフスタイルも価値観もすっかり欧米化、いや無国籍化したコスモポリタンになったつもりの日本人が多い。しかし、客観的にみれば、相変わらず「日本人的」なのである。

These were just a part of the incidents that happened around November 2017. Although most Japanese may not have noticed, **those incidents are very uniquely Japanese on both a historical and cultural standpoint**. They would be difficult for foreigners to understand without the detailed explanation about the background. It seems that many Japanese regard themselves as global persons as their lifestyles and values have become westernized in the 21st century. Considered objectively, however, Japanese people are still "very Japanese."

CHAPTER 3

日常生活やカジュアルな光景に見るタブー

Taboos in everyday life and at casual occasions

訪日観光客が約 2870 万人、日本で働く外国人労働者も 127 万人を超え、留学生・**実習生**も前年比 25%で伸びている。こうして日本人が外国人と接する機会が増えてくるにしたがって、日本人の習慣や価値観と、異文化で育ってきた彼／彼女らとの**食い違いによる摩擦やトラブル**も日常化している。入浴の仕方、花見のエチケット、ゴミ捨てのルールなど、観光地には**外国人向けの注意書き**がやたらと目立つようになってきた。「日本に来たら、その習慣やルールを尊重し、守って欲しい」と言いたくなるのは自然な人情であるが、それぞれにとっての譲れないタブーが衝突する場合は問題が複雑になる。

日本では、日常の些細な行動、動作のことを“箸の上げ下ろし”というが、ここでは、その“**箸の上げ下ろし**”レベルの、双方の言い分や考え方を見てみよう

About 28.7 million tourists come to Japan, more than 1.27 million foreign people work here, and the number of foreign students and **technical interns** has increased 25% from the previous year. As the opportunities where Japanese and foreigner's interaction increase, we see more **frictions and troubles between them because of the differences** of customs and values that they have as backgrounds. We see more and more **notices for foreigners** at tourist spots explaining the proper way of bathing, the etiquette of the cherry blossom viewing, the rules of garbage disposal, and so on. For Japanese, it is natural that they want foreigners to respect the customs and rules of Japan while in Japan. But when it comes to the taboos that both Japanese and foreigners can't compromise, the situation will get complicated.

The Japanese expression "**the way you use the chopsticks**" means the way people act and do small stuff in everyday life. Let's take a look at each party's thinking of small stuff in life.

ハラール、コーシャ、ベジーへの対応

日本の観光地で、外国人にも飲食を提供する人たちが、今、一番勉強しているのが、「ハラール、コーシャ、ベジー」への対応である。ハラール（HALAL）は、イスラム教徒（ムスリム）が守る**食事の戒律**で、不浄な豚肉、血抜きしてない肉、アルコールは「ハラム（禁じられたもの）」になる。厳密にはムスリムが経典にのっとって浄化したものに限られる。また、コーシャ（KOSHER）は、ユダヤ教徒向けの食事の戒律で、やはり豚肉を食べない。食べて良い肉は草食で、割れた蹄を持ち、**反芻する**こと。魚はヒレとウロコのあるもの。肉と乳製品は一緒に食べない。酒は禁じていない。などのルールがあり、やはり戒律に沿って正しく処理されていることが**前提**になる。

ハラールもコーシャも、現在は国際的な**認証機関**があり、日本でも原材料メーカーや飲食店で認証を受け、シールなどで明示しているところも増えた。スープや肉に豚を使わず、鶏肉ベースで作る「ハラール　ラーメン」専門店もできている。これは、インドネシアのようにイスラム教の国からの来日が増えているからだ。コーシャへの対応も急がれているのは、欧米で「コーシャ認定」の食材というのは概ね安全かつヘルシーだというので、ユダヤ教徒ではないが、**意識の高い層や富裕層**などに好まれているからだ。

Dealing with halal, kosher, and veggie

The people who offer food and drink to foreigners at tourist spots in Japan are now eagerly studying halal, kosher and veggie. Halal is Muslim **dietary law**. Pork is non-halal, so is meat with blood and alcoholic beverages. The strict definition of halal is the food adheres to Islamic law as defined in the Koran. Kosher is the food that satisfies the requirements of Jewish law. Its rules are as follows: Pork is forbidden as well and for land animals, any creature that eats grass, has split hooves and **chews its cud** is kosher. For fish that has both fins and scales is kosher. To eat meat and milk together is prohibited. Alcoholic beverages are permitted. The **prerequisite** is that the food should be "blessed by a rabbi."

There are international **certification authorities** of halal and kosher food now. The increasing number of raw material makers and restaurants get the certifications and show them either on the seals or in some other way. There are ramen noodle restaurants specialized in "halal ramen," in which the soup is chicken based, and no pork or meat is used, as the number of Islam tourists is increasing such as Indonesian. Dealing with Kosher food is an urgent matter because "kosher certified" food is regarded as healthy in Western countries, and it has a high demand by **intellectual and rich** non-Jewish **people**.

最後の「ベジー(Veggie)」はベジタリアン(菜食主義者)で「ビーガン(Vegan)」ともいう。日本でもマクロビオテック(Macrobiotic)な食事をする人が増えているが、専門レストランはまだ少ない。動物性食品や調味料などで **“コンタミ(汚染)”** されていたら、彼／彼女らは受け付けない。だから大豆グルテンで肉の触感を出す禅料理などに人気がある。外国人観光客の中に、禅宗の寺の宿坊に泊まる人も、楽しみは「**精進料理**」だという。ビーガン向けに、野菜だけを使えば良いかというとそう簡単ではない。「**有機栽培(オーガニック)**」限定なのである。

世界には、宗教や習慣、信条による独自の食文化がたくさんある。それに接する機会が増えたことによって、料理や材料を変え、物流を変え、栽培や飼育、醸造などの生産現場まで変えようとしている。これまで**アレルギー対策**の面でさまざまな改善はなされてきたが、今起きている3分野の取り組みはその規模を上回り、“食のSCM(サプライチェーン・マネジメント)革命”になりつつある。これは日本にとって、大変な負担かもしれないが、自分たちが慣習的に続けてきた食文化を改めて見直すきっかけになっている点では大きな意義がある。悪いことではない。

The last one, veggie, means vegetarian and is also called as vegan. The number of people who like macrobiotics is increasing, but there are only a few macrobiotic restaurants in Japan. The macrobiotic people will not accept the food if it is "**contaminated**" by animal products or seasonings containing animal products. That is why Zen cooking, which includes soy gluten that has the texture of meat, is popular. Foreign tourists staying at Zen temples look forward to having the **vegetarian dishes called *shōjin ryōri***. For vegans, dishes in which only vegetables are used are not enough. The vegetables must be "**organically certified**."

There are various food cultures in the world based on religions, customs or beliefs. The Japanese have more opportunities to deal with those cultures now, so they are trying to change cooking methods and materials, food distribution systems, and production sites of farming and brewing. In the past, various improvements have been made for **countermeasures against allergies**, but the measures for these three fields have bigger sales, and it is becoming a "Supply Chain Management (SCM) revolution." It might be a big burden for Japan, but, at the same time, it could be a good opportunity for us to rethink our own conventional food culture. It's not a negative thing.

日本人だけが好む「八重歯」

食事に繋がる話となると、体との関係だ。食後に歯磨きする習慣を持つ人が多いのは**虫歯や歯周病予防**も考えるからだが、その際、自分の**歯の白さや歯並び**を気にする人もいるだろう。見た目の印象を大きく左右することを経験的に知るからだ。その歯並びだが、日本人の若い女性たちの間では「**八重歯**」が“可愛い〜！”とされる。「八重」とは花びらや人垣がいくつも重なっている状態を指す。歯が重なる原因は、アゴの骨が小さくて、**乳歯から永久歯に変わる**時に生え変わるスペースがなくなり、永久歯が外側に押し出されてしまうことによる。

口の端っこに見えるこの「八重歯」が“可愛い〜！”と思われてきたのは、少女期から大人になるくらいの齢に、「まだ完全ではない子供らしさ」の象徴と見た人が多かったからだろう。しかし、これを“可愛い〜！”なんて言うのは日本人だけである。海外、とくに欧米では、幼い時から歯並びを徹底的に矯正する。**育ちが悪く、貧しく、教養が無い**とみなされてしまうからだ。矯正用マウスピースや金属製の矯正具をした子どもをたくさん見かける。

でも、矯正中の子どもたちだってずいぶん恥ずかしい思いをしているに違いない。アニメ映画『トイ・ストー

Only Japanese adores "double tooth"

Food gives nutrition to the body. Many people have a habit of brushing their teeth after meals to **prevent cavity and gum disease**. And some people might pay attention to **teeth color and alignment** as they know that the appearance of their teeth is important to the impression of their appearance. Japanese young women think that ***yaeba*** **(double tooth)** is cute. By the way, *yae* means many layers of flower petals or a crowd of people. The cause of the double tooth is the small jaw bones; when **a milk tooth changes to a permanent tooth**, there is not enough space for a permanent tooth to grow, and it is pushed out as a result.

I think the reason why the Japanese people regard the double tooth as a cute thing is that we see it as a kind of reminiscence of childhood during the transition period from a girl to a woman. But only Japanese think the double tooth is cute. In other countries, especially in the Western world, parents make their children wear braces on their teeth to have their teeth straightened. Irregular teeth are regarded as **ill-bread, poor, and illiterate**. So, we see many children with orthodontic mouthpieces or metal braces.

But those children must be having a tough time. In an animation movie "Toy Story," Sid with badly aligned

リー』に出てくる歯並びの汚いシドは**悪役**であるし、同じく『ファインディング・ニモ』に登場する歯科医の娘ドーラも、ワイヤー矯正中で意地悪な性格に描かれている。近年は、日本でも**歯科美容や予防歯科**の考え方が普及するようになり、「八重歯」のままであることを恥ずかしいと思う人も増えてきた。

「八重歯は個性的」なんて話は、他の国では通じない。歯医者を儲けさせるつもりはないが、「即、矯正すべき」という流れを加速するには、日本人男性たちの**美意識**から変えるしかない。あるネット調査によると、「八重歯を可愛いと思う」男性が73.6%もいるのである。

teeth is depicted as a **villain** and Dory in "Finding Nemo," a dentist's daughter with an orthodontic wire, is portrayed as mean spirited. Recently even in Japan, **cosmetic and preventive dentistry** are becoming popular, and many people have started to think the double tooth is embarrassing.

If you say, "The double tooth is an expression of personality," people would not understand it in other countries. I'm not trying to make orthodontists profitable, but to make the trend of correcting double tooth more popular, we have to start from changing the Japanese males' **sense of beauty**. According to a survey on the Internet, 73.6% males still think that double tooth is cute.

日本人でもとまどう、「上座」「下座」

料亭などで会食する際に、**偉い人や年長者**に対して「どうぞ**上座へ**」と案内している光景を見たことがあると思う。そう、日本人の間では、「どの席に座るか」にれっきした上下のヒエラルキー（階層秩序）がある。一般的な座敷では、花や掛け軸で置かれる“**床の間**”の前が上座であり、それがない場合でも入り口から遠くの落ち着く席が上座になる。そこから左右に、そして入り口に向かうほど「下座」になる。新人や若い人などが座ることが多い。

別に上座に座ったからといって、特別メニューにはならないし、料理を美味しく感ずるわけでもない。人間関係における、たぶんに**儒教的なヒエラルキー**を、この会食の場でも尊重しますという参加者の**暗黙の合意**に過ぎない。日本人でもとまどうことがあるのだ。

「上座」「下座」は料亭だけにあるのではない。会議の席、タクシーの座席、エレベーター内の立ち位置にもある。それなりの合理性を持つケースもあるが、多くは「誰が決めたんだ！」と怒りたくなるような慣習である。**儒教文化の名残り**だから、その影響が日本以上に大きい韓国では、

Seating etiquettes that even Japanese get confused about

You might have seen, at a traditional Japanese restaurant, that a **high-ranking or elderly person** is guided to ***kami-za* (the position of greater honor)**. As you have guessed, there is a clear hierarchy whether to take one's place in a position of greater or lesser honor. In a typical Japanese style room, the place of highest honor is that close to the ***tokonoma* alcove** where flowers or hanging scrolls are displayed. If there is no *tokonoma*, it is the furthest and most comfortable place from the entrance. The next high order is the left and right of the highest honor place. The closer to the entrance, the lesser (*shimo-za*) the place becomes. Often, a newcomer or young person sits there.

Even if you sit in the position of greater honor, it doesn't mean that you can get a special menu or the food tastes better. It is just an **unspoken agreement** among the diners that they respect the **Confucian hierarchy** in the room. Even Japanese get confused sometimes.

The place of greater or lesser honor applies to the seating arrangement at a meeting, in a taxi, and where to stand in an elevator. In some cases, it is reasonable. But in most cases, this custom is very annoying. This is a **trace of the Confucian culture** in Japan. But in

日本よりもはるかに「上下関係、年齢の長幼関係」に厳しい。

（詳しく知りたい方は、私の著書『ニッポンのしきたり』（IBCパブリッシング）に図解したので、そちらを見て欲しい。PRである）

Korea, where Confucianism has a deep effect in its culture, the hierarchy of the ranks and ages is stricter than in Japan.

(If you want to know more about this subject, please refer to my book “Customs of Japan” published by IBC Publishing.)

おかしな、おかしな「敬語」の使い方

シチュエーションに応じた言葉の使い分けの典型的なものが「**敬語**」だろう。敬語には形式がある。相手に敬意を示す「尊敬語」、相手よりへりくだる言い方の「謙譲語」、より丁寧な言い方をする時の「丁寧語」の3種類の形式だ。でも接客サービスの現場や若い人たちの間でも正確に使いこなすことが難しくて、この使い分けがおかしくなっている。

取引先の相手や上司から示された書類を見る時に、「**拝見させていただきます**」というが、「拝見」というのは自分の動作である「見る」の謙譲語、「いただく」は「する」の謙譲語だから2重に敬語を使っていることになる。シンプルに「拝見します」が正しい。また、ファミレスなどでアルバイトのウェイターが、注文内容を繰り返すことがあるが、最後に「……(品名)で、よろしかったでしょうか?」と確認する。丁寧さを強調しているつもりが、過去形になっているために、無言のうちに「以上で注文は終わりね(the end of your order)」と仕切られた感じを与えている。もちろんアルバイトの当人は気づかない。どうしても確認したければ「……(品名)で、よろしいですか?」で良いはずだ。他にも、**相手**からとくに依頼されていないのに、「……(動作)させていただきます」もおかしい。相手が「……(動作)してほしい」と依頼したことへの言葉なら正しい。さらに、「お机」とか「お名刺」など、やたら

Strange honorific expressions

A typical example of word usage depending on the situations is ***keigo* (honorific expressions)**. There are three kinds of honorific expressions: *sonkei-go* (an honorific language) to express respect to another party, *kenjō-go* (a humble language) to express a humbleness, and *teinei-go* (a polite language) to speak politely. It is, however, difficult to use them correctly, and customer service professionals or young people are having a hard time using them appropriately.

When taking a look at a document shown by a client or a superior, Japanese people would say, "***Haiken sasete itadakimasu.* (I will duly take a look at the document you handed to me**.)" *Haiken* is a humble form of *miru* (look) as it is your action, and *itadaku* is also a humble form of *suru* (do), and so there are redundant honorific expressions in this sentence. The correct way of saying it is simply "*Haiken shimasu.*" At a family restaurant, when part-time waiters confirm the customers' order, they say, "*Xxx* (the dish name) *de yoroshikatta deshouka*? (*Xxx* was your order, wasn't it?)" They say it in this way to express politeness. But by using the past tense, it sounded like "It is the end of your order and no more." The waiters are not aware of how it sounds. If they want to confirm the order, they can simply say, "*Xxx* (the dish name) *de yoroshii desuka*? (*Xxx* is your order,

と丁寧語の**接頭語「お」**を付けたがるのもおかしい。これらが新人への**教育マニュアル**に書かれているというから驚く。

かくして「おかしな、おかしな敬語」は**蔓延**するばかり。日本人でも間違うのだから、外国人に完璧な「敬語」を求めるのは、もう無理な話だ。

isn't it?)" Another wrong usage of honorific expression is "*xxx* (action) *sasete itadaki-masu* (let me duly do *xxx* for you)" when the **other party** is not asking you to do anything. If someone is asking you to do something in particular, this expression is fine, though. Another example is a **prefix *o*** that indicates politeness. Adding *o* in front of *tsukue* (desk) or *meishi* (business card) is wrong. Surprisingly, I heard that these wrong usages are recommended in the **educational manual** for new employees.

In this way, strange honorific expressions are **spreading widely**. Even Japanese can't use them correctly, so you can't expect foreigners to use them perfectly.

残念な結果になるコミュニケーション

言葉はコミュニケーションの大事な道具である。一生懸命にそれぞれの外国語を話そうとしても残念な結果を招くリスクもある。外国人が日本語を上手く使えなくても、「ガイジンだから」と許されることが多いが、少し英語を話せる日本人が、変な言葉を使って、違和感を与える場合も増えている。日本人は、英語表現のとくに**形容詞**の使い分けが苦手なのだ。

たとえば、「マジメな人ね」と**褒めたくて**、辞書にある「serious」とか「square」を使っても、喜ぶ外国人は少ない。「**くそマジメ**で面白くない」「**頭の固いやつ**」というニュアンスがあるからだ。「行動的、積極的」と言いたくて「aggressive」と言う日本人も多いが、「攻撃的でガツガツしている」というニュアンスに気づかない。

逆に、日本人の若い女の子とばかり会話して、「**オネエ言葉**」の日本語を使っていることに気づかない外国人もいる。おかしな**流行語**に染まることも要注意だ。たとえば彼女たちは、すぐに「ヤバイ！」と言う。本来なら「Oh dear」と同じく、「危険な状態だ」という意味なのだが、彼女たちは「おいしい」も、「美しい」も、「すてき」も、すべて「ヤバイ！」ですませてしまう。これには、年配者た

Poor communication

Language is an important communication tool. When you try hard to speak in a foreign language, sometimes it has a risk to cause regretful results. When foreigners speak poor Japanese, Japanese people would not mind it so much because they are *gaijin*. But opposite cases are increasing; Japanese people with poor English use strange words and make native speakers wonder. Japanese are usually not good at using **adjectives** in particular.

For example, Japanese people often use the words "serious" or "square" when they **intend to praise** someone as "diligent." It will not be taken as pleasant expressions by foreigners because "serious" or "square" are used to describe someone as "**inflexible** and not interesting" or "**stubborn**." Many Japanese use the adjective "aggressive" that has a nuance of "offensive and greedy" when they want to say, "active or positive."

On the contrary, there are foreigners who don't know that they are using "**women's words**" as they learned Japanese by speaking with young girls only. Using **vogue words** among girls is difficult as well. For example, they often say "*Yabai*!" in Japanese. Originally, it is used when the situations are dangerous like "Oh, dear!" But for them, it could mean many things such as

ちは「眉をひそめる」(＝嫌がる)。また彼女たちは、何かを食べて、「美味しい」という普通の言葉があるのに、「ウマッ！」(旨い) と言うのが口癖になっている。男性でもかなり下品、**くだけ過ぎた**言い方であることを周囲の大人たちが注意しないからだ。(どうも、私の話は頑固な老人の繰り言になってしまう。ヤバイ！)

いや、言葉だけではない。ジェスチャーやハンドサインにもリスクが伴う。たとえば、**親指と人差し指で丸く輪を作る**サインが、日本では「OK」と「お金」の両方の意味があること。同じくハンドサインでは、「小指」を立てるのは「女性」や「恋人」の意味であること……等々、国によってはとても危ないハンドサインが横行している。旅行ハンドブックやYouTubeでも、これらのすべてが分かるわけではないから、お互いに違和感を持つかもしれない。

tasty, beautiful or nice. For this kind of word selection, elderly people would *mayu wo hisomeru* (knit their brow or frown). Also, young girls would say "*Uma*!" instead of *oishii* (tasty) when they eat something good because the adults around them don't teach them that *umai* is usually used by vulgar men and **too casual** for girls. (Well, I'm talking like an old man. *Yabai*!)

Not only words but also gestures and hand signs have risks. For example, in Japan, **making a circle by thumb and an index finger** means "OK" or "money," and making little finger up means "woman" or "lover." These hand signs could mean something different in other countries and could be dangerous to use them. You can't learn everything about gestures or hand signs in various countries from travel guidebooks or YouTube, so we have to be aware that different gestures could mean different things in different countries.

「大安」を喜び、「仏滅」を嫌う

日本のカレンダーや**手帳**を見ると、日付に添えて小さく「先勝」、「友引」、「先負」、「仏滅」、「大安」、「赤口」の6種類の文字が書かれている。これを「六曜」と言い、**日取りの吉凶**を占う目安としてきた。いや、過去形ではない。21世紀でも現在進行形なのである。「六曜」は、由来もはっきりせず、それぞれの解釈も、**時代によって変遷してきた**のに、近世になるほど形が定まって普及し、人々が日常の中に取り入れてきた。

「六曜」がどう違うかを簡単に書くと以下の通り。

- 先勝（せんしょう）：早めに事を運ぶと縁起が良いが午後は凶。
- 友引（ともびき）：「友人を引き入れる」から**慶事**に良いが**弔事**はNO！
- 先負（せんぶ）：「先勝」の正反対。午前は凶で、午後は吉。
- 仏滅（ぶつめつ）：「仏が滅する」の意味で何事も凶の日。
- 大安（たいあん）：すべてにおいて良い結果が得られる吉の日。
- 赤口（しゃっこう）：新しいことは避けて何事にも慎む日。

Love *taian* (the luckiest day) and hate *butsumetsu* (the unluckiest day)

On Japanese calendars or **day planners**, in addition to the dates, six kinds of letters are written such as 先勝 (*senshō*), 友引 (*tomobiki*), 先負 (*senbu*), 仏滅 (*butsumetsu*), 大安 (*taian*) and 赤口 (*shakkō*). They are called *rokuyō*, and they were used to determine **lucky and unlucky days**. Actually, the past tense is not correct, as it is still used in the 21st century as well. The origin of *rokuyō* is unclear, and its interpretation has been **changing as time has gone by**. But in the early modern period, their meanings were fixed and it became important in everyday life.

The explanation of *rokuyō* is as follows:

Senshō: If you do things early, it is lucky, but the afternoon is unlucky.

Tomobiki: It literally means "Bring in your friends." So, it is lucky for **fortunate events** but not good for a **funeral**.

Senbu: Opposite of *Senshō*. Morning is unlucky, but the afternoon is lucky.

Butsumetsu: It means "the day of Buddha's death." The unluckiest day.

Taian: The luckiest day for everything.

Shakkō: Avoid new things and be discreet with everything.

ということで、結婚式場の利用率を調べたある結婚コンサルティングサイトによると、おめでたいとされる「大安」と「友引」の日の利用率が合計で40%、縁起が悪い「仏滅」の日は嫌われてわずか6%に留まる。葬儀についてのデータはないが、**葬儀屋**は「友引」の**通夜**は避けるべきとアドバイスするし、**火葬場**も休日にしているところが多い。死者が仲間を引き込むという解釈が優勢だからだ。

他にも「六曜」は、お祝いを買う、届ける、見舞いに行く、引っ越し、納車、家を建てる、宝くじの購入、新しい鞄や靴を使い始めるなどで**日取り**の参考にする人がいる。

しかし、ほとんどの人は、今日が「六曜」の何に当たるかを知らないし、気にもしていない。仏教でも占いを否定しているくらいだ。古い習慣を守る年寄り世代や**冠婚葬祭**を商いにしている専門家、占い師などが助言して初めて考慮し、参考にする程度である。ちなみに「六曜」発祥の地とされてきた中国にはこんな習慣はない。中国発祥説に根拠はない。

According to a wedding consulting web site, a survey of bridal halls usage showed that 40% of the wedding ceremonies took place on the lucky days of *taian* and *tomobiki*, and only 6% on the unlucky day of *butsumetsu*. There is no such data available for funerals, but **undertakers** advise that **wakes** on *tomobiki* days should be avoided. Most **crematories** are closed on those days as it is believed that the dead will call for more people on *tomobiki* days.

Other than weddings and funerals, some people take *rokuyō* into consideration when they **decide the dates** for buying and sending gifts, visiting someone in the hospital, moving, delivering new vehicles, building a house, buying lotteries, and starting to use a new bag or wear new shoes.

But most people don't know the *rokuyō* of the day or don't even care about it. Fortune telling is denied in Buddhism. Most people will not take *rokuyō* into consideration until they get advice from older generations who keep the old customs, the specialists of **weddings or funerals**, and fortune tellers. By the way, there are no such customs in China where *rokuyō* is believed to have originated from, and there is no foundation for that theory.

似たような「**縁起かつぎ**」は世界中にたくさんある。数字でいえば、キリスト教圏では「13」や「666」が嫌われ、日本では「4（死）」や「9（苦）」が嫌われる。アフガニスタンでは「39」が**ポン引き**や売春婦を意味する数字だとの説があるが、由来も**真偽**も不明だ。

There are similar **superstitions** all over the world. When we look at numbers, 13 or 666 is avoided in the countries where Christianity is believed. Four (pronounced as *shi* in Japanese, which is the same sound as "death") and nine (pronounced as *ku* in Japanese, which is the same sound as "hardship") are unlucky numbers in Japan. A theory says that 39 means **pimps** and prostitutes in Afghanistan, but its origin and **authenticity** are not clear.

着物の襟が左右反対だと笑われるわけ

数年前のことだが、ある女性タレントがブログに自分の浴衣姿の写真をアップして**“炎上”した**ことがあった。彼女が襟の向きを左右逆にして着ていたからだ。彼女は「画像を**反転**しただけよ」と言い訳したが、そうする動機に説得力がない。明らかに間違えたのだろう。ブログの記事は騒動後すぐに消去された。

着物では、着ている人の体寄り（内側）を「前」という。V字状に左右の襟を重ねる際には、右側が前（体寄り）つまり「右前」に着なくてはならない。これは男女とも同じである。洋服では、男性用は右前なのに女性用は左前に作られているから外国人や若い女性が間違うことが多い。日本で「左前」は、**死装束**に用いられるだけである。

この「左前」を嫌う習慣は中国から来たもので、**中華文明の圏外に住む野蛮な民族**の衣装とみなされていたとの説がある。この理由以外にも、「左前」だと右利きには財布の出し入れがしにくいことから、「お金が入ってこない」、つまり「左前＝お金がない」の意味にも使われる。ともかく、この格好で街を歩いたら笑われることになるから要注意である。

The left or right flap of kimono matters

Several years ago, a female entertainer posted her pictures in *yukata* (casual cotton kimono for summer), and **got flamed** for it because she had worn her *yukata* with the left flap next to the skin. Her excuse was that the picture had been the **reverse** image, but it was not persuasive. It was apparent that she had made a mistake. The blog article was removed right after the squall.

When wearing a kimono, the part touching the body is called *mae* (front). To make a V shape with the right and left flaps, the right flap (as seen by someone facing you) should be *mae* (front) and close to the body. This is the same for both men and women. With the western-style clothing, women's style is opposite. So, foreigners or young Japanese easily make mistakes when wearing a kimono. In Japan, wearing a kimono with the left side front is only for **burial clothes**.

This custom of hating clothing with left flap side front is said to have originated in China where it is regarded as the custom of **barbarian ethnic groups outside of Chinese culture**. Another reason for this custom is because it is inconvenient for right-handed people to get their wallet out, and it lead to wearing left flap front means "no money." In any case, if you wear a

着物について追加しよう。優雅な長い袖のついた「振り袖」は人気がある。しかし、これはあくまで若い**未婚の女性**が着るものである。既婚女性は袖の短い「留め袖」である。

kimono with left flap side front, you would be laughed at for sure. Be careful.

Another caution about the kimono; *Furisode*, an elegant long-sleeved kimono, is very popular, but it should only be worn by **unmarried women**. Married women wear *tomesode* that has shorter sleeves.

ローカルな敵対意識が残る面白さ

イングランド人が嫌いなスコットランド人、ヤンキー(北軍)が嫌いなテキサス人(南軍)という具合に、一つの国の中にも歴史的に形成されたライバル心、敵対意識がある。サッカーのダービー・マッチでは、一つの町が**2分**される騒ぎになる。

日本でも、福島県・会津地方では、鹿児島県(旧国名薩摩)や山口県(同長州)の人を悪く言う人が多かった。徳川幕府側だった会津を**官軍**側の薩摩・長州が攻めたからだ。しかしその隣の山形は薩摩に好印象を持つ人が多かった。やはり明治維新の際、幕府側に立った山形(米沢藩)に対して、薩摩の西郷隆盛が寛大な処遇をしてくれたからだといわれる。穏やかな南国に思える沖縄でも、昔の**琉球王朝**と八重山諸島とは激しく戦った歴史がある。

もっとミクロにみれば、青森の津軽地方と南部地方(一部は岩手県)なども歴史的な背景があるが、もっと「**コップの中の嵐**」みたいな、ささやかなライバル心、敵対意識はどこにでもある。静岡と浜松、新潟と長岡、富山と高岡……同一県内の**県庁所在地**とNo. 2の対抗意識が見られる。**他県人**が外から見たら大した問題には見えなくても、

Local rivalry remains

Englishmen hate Irishmen and Texans (Confederate) hate Yankees (Union). As such, there are historically formed rivalries even within a country. At a Derby match of soccer, a town is **divided in two**, and it turns into big uproar.

In Japan, many people from Aizu in Fukushima prefecture used to speak badly about the people from Kagoshima prefecture (former Satsuma clan) and Yamaguchi prefecture (former Chōshū clan). It is because the **government army** of Satsuma and Chōshū attacked Aizu which was Tokugawa Shogunate side. But in Yamagata prefecture next to Aizu, many people had good impressions about the Satsuma people. It is said that, at the Meiji Restoration, Takamori Saigō of Satsuma treated Yamagata (former Yonezawa clan) people well. Okinawa seems to be a peaceful southern country, but it has a history of fierce fighting between the **Ryūkyū Dynasty** and Yaeyama Islands.

If we look closer, Tsugaru and southern regions in Aomori prefecture (part of its southern region belongs to Iwate prefecture) have a historic background. But minor rivalries like "**storm in a teacup**" can be seen in everywhere. Shizuoka and Hamamatsu, Niigata and Nagaoka, and Toyama and Takaoka are examples

当地の人にしたら、デリケートな問題だったりする。

筆者が経験した一例。山形県では秋になると収穫した里芋を鍋料理にして、**河川敷**などで大勢で楽しむ「芋煮会」が名物だ。海岸寄りの庄内地方では、里芋に豚肉を加えて味噌味で仕立てる。しかし置賜・村山地方では、牛肉で醤油味である。もっと細かくいうと、最上地方は寄せ鍋風にする。こういう「芋煮の常識」を知らないままに、「山形の芋煮は旨いですね。牛肉とよく合って……」と、庄内地方の人に話したところ、露骨にイヤな顔をされた。

地方にいったら、その土地の人が**対抗**心を持つ地域のことをまず知るべきだ。そしてその優劣をどう論じているかも知るべきだ。その**予備知識**なしに**不用意な発言**をするのは**「地雷」を踏む**ことになる。ま、これはこれで面白いのだが……。

of the rivalries between the **prefectural capital** and a similar sized No. 2 city in the same prefecture. From the **people outside those prefectures**, the problem is not so serious. But for the people in those cities, it is a delicate matter.

Let me share with you an example that I have experienced. In Yamagata Prefecture, an *imoni kai* party is famous where people bring the autumn harvest of taro and cook them in pots at **river beds**. At Shōnai area near the beach, they cook taro and pork together in miso (fermented soybean) soup. But in Okitama and Murayama regions, they add beef and cook in soy sauce based soup. To be more precise, in Mogami region, taro is cooked with several other ingredients. Without knowing the "common knowledge of *imoni*," I talked to a person from Shōnai region. "Yamagata's *imoni* is very good. It goes very well with beef…" The person apparently made a face at me.

If you go to local areas, the first thing you have to know is the **rivalries** between certain areas, and also what the disputing points are. Without knowing that **background information** and if you make **thoughtless remarks**, you will end up **stepping on a land mine**. Well, if that happens, it would be kind of interesting in its own way…

　ちなみに、その地方が歴史的・地理的背景を踏まえて、どのように**区分け**されているかを知る方法は、ローカルな天気予報を見るのが便利である。新潟県を例に挙げると、「上越」(主に南西部)、「中越」(中央部)、「下越」(県都・新潟市を含む北東部)、「佐渡」の４つに区分して天気予報が出される。これは、言葉や習慣などの違いも含めておおむね分かりやすい区分になっている。

For your information, the good way to know the **division** of a local area based on its historical and geographic background is to watch the local weather forecast. For example, the weather forecast of Niigata prefecture is divided into four areas: Jōetsu (mainly south west region), Chūetsu (central region), Kaetsu (north east region including Niigata city, the prefectural capital) and Sado. These divisions are easy to understand including the differences of language and custom.

CHAPTER 4

消えるタブーと増えるタブー

Disappearing taboos and increasing taboos

あらためて「タブー」とは何かを考えてみる。日本の代表的な辞書である『広辞苑』では、その語源を、ポリネシア語で「『聖なる』の意の tabu、tapu から」と説明したうえで、「**超自然的**な危険な力を持つ事柄に対して、社会的に厳しく禁止される特定の行為。触れたり口に出したりしてはならないとされる物・事柄。**禁忌**。」とある。たしかに、狩猟の掟や婚姻、資産の相続、協働作業など共同体を営む上でこうしたタブーは必要だった。だが、そのすべてが合理的なものではなかったし、時代や**構成員**の変化とともに変わってきた。近代的な法治国家では、法律などで**明文化**されるものも多い。タブーの多くは変化するものといえる。

本書でここまで見てきたのは、さまざまなルールや、暗黙のうちに順守している慣習など、現在の日本社会で見出せる**広義**の、「タブー」である。このパートでは、少しハードなテーマを取り上げ、消えゆく部分と増える部分があることを考えてみたい。実は、筆者である私は、こういう**奥の深い**、大きな問題を語るのは苦手である。庶民の、安逸な暮らしの中で**小さな事象**だけで十分なのだ。大問題を語ることこそ自分にとっての「タブー」と思う。しかし、小事を語って大事を避けるのでは、読者が許すまい。そこで、筆者なりに取り上げてみることにする。

Once again, I'd like to think about what a taboo means. According to a famous Japanese dictionary Kōjien, the origin of the word "taboo" is explained as follows: "It came from a Polynesian word '*tabu*' or '*tapu*' which means 'sacred.'" "Certain actions socially strictly forbidden against things that have **supernatural** and dangerous power. Things or matters that are not supposed to be touched or talked about. **Prohibition**." For the community that had hunting rules, marriage, inheritance, and collaborative work, taboos were necessary for sure. But not all the taboos were rational, and they have been altered with the times and the changes of the **people in the community**. In modern constitutional states, many taboos are **stipulated**. It can be said that most of the taboos change.

Up to here, I've written about the taboos in a **broad sense** of the word such as various rules and silently observed customs in current Japanese society. In this part, I'd like to pick up slightly tougher themes, and thorough them examine the increasing and disappearing parts of taboos. To be honest, I'm not good at writing about such an **in-depth**, large subject. It would be nice if I could stick with the **small stuff** in peaceful everyday life. To talk about big problems is kind of "taboo" for me. But for my readers, I will write about these large matters in my own way.

性的少数者に対する偏見はどうなる？

東京・新宿の「2丁目」には、ゲイなど**性的少数者**の人たちが集まるバーやクラブがたくさんある。増えてきた外国人観光客も加わって、その界隈は毎晩にぎわっている。かつては偏見で見られ、差別や意地悪を受けてきた彼や彼女たちマイノリティも、ここではのびのびと明るく過ごしている。日本の「LGBT**解放区**」の感さえある。

「LGBT」は、レズビアン（女性同性愛者）の「L」、ゲイ（男性同性愛者）の「G」、バイセクシュアル（両性愛者）の「B」、トランスジェンダー（心と体の性が一致しない人）の「T」の頭文字をとったセクシュアルマイノリティ（性的少数者）の総称だ。だがこの4通りだけではない。このどれにも属さない人、たとえば、「インターセックス（I）」＝身体的に男女の区別がつきにくい人や、「アセクシュアル（A）」＝無性愛者。同性も異性も好きにならない人、「クエスチョニング（Q）」＝自分の性別や**性的指向**に確信が持てない人なども含まれる。人間の「性」は多様なのだ。

その「LGBT」を巡っては、世界でもさまざまな動きが起きている。映画『ムーンライト』は、ゲイの黒人青年の半生を描いたものだが、2016年のアカデミー賞作品賞を受賞した。台湾ではアジア初の**同性婚**を認める判決が出た。日本でも2015年に東京・渋谷区が同性カップルに対して事実上の婚姻証明となる**「パートナーシップ証明書」**を交付した（でも、このカップルは、2017年12月に“離

Prejudice against the sexual minorities

At Shinjuku 2-chome in Tokyo, there are many bars and clubs where gay people and **sexual minorities** get together. With the increasing number of tourists, the area is very popular every night. The sexual minorities, who used to be discriminated against and harassed, are enjoying their time here. This area looks almost like Japan's "LGBT **liberated zone**."

"LGBT" stands for Lesbian (a homosexual woman), Gay (homosexual), Bisexual (a person sexually attracted to both men and women) and Transgender (people whose gender identity differs from the sex they were assigned at birth). Sexual minorities also include Intersex (people whose body does not fit the typical definitions for male or female bodies), Asexual (people who are not sexually attracted to either men or women) and Questioning (people who are unsure of their **sexual orientation** or gender identity). There are many varieties of human "sexuality."

Many movements are happening surrounding LGBT. A movie "Moonlight," which depicts the life of a black gay man, won the Academy Award for Best Picture in 2016. In Taiwan, the court approved the **same sex marriage** for the first time in Asia. In Japan, Tokyo's Shibuya ward issued a **same sex partnership paper** recognizing their partnership as equivalent to

婚”して証明書を返上したが……)。後ろ向きな事例では、米国のトランプ政権がトランスジェンダーの米軍内の勤務を禁止した。

では、こうした性的少数者が一体、どれくらい存在するのだろう？　大手広告代理店電通の**関連会社**ダイバーシティ・ラボが、全国の約7万人を対象に**ネット調査**したところ、日本の「LGBT」比率は約7.6%（約1000万人）となった。これは80歳以上の総人口とほぼ同じであり、血液型がAB型の人の数と同じとの説もある。いずれにしても**12人に1人**だからかなり高い比率だ。80歳以上とかAB型なんて人は身近にたくさんいるではないか。彼や彼女のすべてが、性的マイノリティであるとカミングアウトしたわけでもないし、それと分かる外見をしているわけではないから、気づかないだけだ。

「LGBT」をタブー視しないという大きな**潮流**は世界的なものである。人間の「性」の多様性を教えてくれるものであり、ごく身近に存在し、問題なく**共生**できると考える人が増えてくれば、このテーマはタブー視されなくなる。

marriage. (Unfortunately, this couple got a "divorce" and returned the paper to the ward office in December 2017.) An example, running counter to the times, President Trump has banned transgender people from US military service.

How many sexual minorities exist in Japan? Diversity LAB, an **affiliate company** of Dentsu, that is one of the largest advertising agencies in Japan, conducted an **Internet survey** on 70,000 people throughout Japan. According to the survey, LGBT people account for 7.6% (about 10 million people) of the Japanese population. This is approximately the same number of the population 80 years or older, and some say that the number is equal to that of people whose blood type is AB. Either way, it is **one out of 12 people**, and the ratio is very high. If you look around, there are many people who are 80 years or older or people whose blood type is AB. We just can't tell who is LGBT because not all the sexual minorities are coming out, and their appearances don't give us much of an idea.

The world **trend** is going in the direction where LGBT is no longer regarded as a taboo. LGBT teaches us the diversities of human "sexuality." This theme will not be regarded as a taboo anymore if the number of people, who think that LGBT people are among us and we can **live together** with them, increases in Japan.

「女性活用」政策のための和製英語？

「性」の問題に関連する話題だが、世界的には、**社会的に弱い立場の人**を是正する改善措置をすべきだとの潮流が主流になっている。そのためには、進学や就職や職場における昇進などに際して、敢えて（ポジティブに）**被差別集団を優遇する措置**も必要になる。これは、昔から「アファーマティブ・アクション（affirmative action）」と呼ばれる。米国の大学における黒人学生の一定数の受け入れなどがその代表例だろう。

日本の厚生労働省では、この対象を女性とし、女性の**社会的参画**を増やす取組みを続けている。だが、現状はなかなか成果が見えない。英国の『エコノミスト』誌が、2017年3月に発表した「**ガラスの天井指数**」という調査によると、日本の女性の活躍度合いは、経済協力開発機構（OECD）加盟国29カ国中の28位。上位にはアイスランドや北欧諸国が並び、日本の下（最下位）につけたのは韓国となっている。「ガラスの天井指数」とは奇妙なネーミングだが、これは「ガラスの天井」つまり「女性の社会進出を妨げる見えない障壁」を指している。そして調査は、男女の高等教育や、労働力率、賃金や育児費用など10項目を加重平均して算出したものだという。たしかに日本は、**管理職**に就く女性の比率が低く、年収の差も大きく、家事

Japanese English made for the "Promotion of Women's Participation and Advancement in the Workplace" policy

Related to the subject of "sexuality," taking improvement measures for **socially vulnerable people** is becoming mainstream worldwide. For that purpose, it becomes necessary to positively take measures of **preferential treatment for the discriminated group** at the occasions such as education, employment, and promotion at the office. This measure has been named "affirmative action." A typical example of the affirmative action is accepting a certain number of black students at universities in the U.S.

Japan's Health, Labor, and Welfare Ministry is continuing its effort to increase women's **involvement in the labor market**. But the situation hasn't changed a lot. "The Economist" magazine in the U.K. presented its "**glass-ceiling index**." According to this survey of women's chances of equal treatment at work, Japan ranked 28 out of the 29 member countries of the Organization for Economic Co-operation and Development (OECD). Nordic countries including Iceland ranked top overall. At the bottom of the ranking was South Korea, which was the only country ranked under Japan. The "glass-ceiling index" sounds strange, but it came from the expression "glass ceiling"

や子育てを女性に押し付ける男性も多い。この結果に関しては、素直に認めるしかないだろう。

「何とかしなくては」と厚生労働省が躍起になっているのは理解する。女性の活躍や男女格差解消を推進して、「2020年までに社会の指導的地位に女性が占める割合を少なくとも30%にする」という目標は立派である。しかし、ちょっとおかしなところもある。

日本の官庁は、政策立案や政策報告の「**白書**」などで、妙な言葉を造語するおかしなクセがある。今回の日本版&女性版「アファーマティブ・アクション（affirmative action）」でも、「ポジティブ・アクション」なる和製英語を創り出した。英語の affirmative action（肯定的措置）と positive discrimination（肯定的差別）を組み合わせて造語したらしい。どうして こんな和製英語を作る必要があるのだろう？　**取り巻きの学者**やシンクタンクのせいかもしれない。

meaning "invisible barrier to prevent women's social advancement." According to The Economist, the survey was conducted combining the data of ten items such as higher education, labor-force participation, pay, and child-care costs. In Japan, for sure, the rate of women **senior managers** is low, the earnings gap between men and women is high, and many men avoid house chores and raising children. So, we have to accept the result of this survey humbly.

It is understandable that the Health, Labor, and Welfare Ministry is trying to improve the situations eagerly. It has an ambitious goal to promote women's active participation in the workplace, to close the gap between the wages of male and female workers, and "to increase the rate of women in management positions to at least 30% by the year 2020." But there is something strange in this goal.

Japanese government offices have a strange habit of creating weird words in their policy making plans or policy report **white papers**. In the Japanese and women's version of "affirmative action" this time, they created Japanese English words "positive action." It must be the combination of the English words "affirmative action" and "positive discrimination." Why did they have to make Japanese English words like this? I wonder if it was made by their **parasite scholars** or their favorite think tank.

世界は「日本の人権状況」に厳しい

「LGBT」を理解する流れが生まれていることを書いたが、日本の「人権状況」全体に対して、世界が厳しい見方をしていることがわかったのは、2017年11月のことである。国連人権理事会が、定期審査で世界106カ国から出た**勧告**をまとめた報告書案を公表し、218もの勧告が記載されたのだ。その中には、韓国・中国・北朝鮮が、「**慰安婦**問題について、歴史の真実に向き合っていない」というものもある。

それ以外にも多かったのは、人種差別や性差別、外国人差別、性的少数者差別などをなくす取り組みに関する勧告で、日本は消極的だというのである。オランダなどが国として「**反差別法**」を制定している動きと比較された。また、報道に対して国が「政治的に公平でない」と介入したとされる。さらに、日本が**死刑制度**を存続させていることに対しても批判的な意見が多い。「法改正が難しければ、死刑執行を一時停止せよ」との勧告もあった。

The world is critical about "Japanese human rights"

I wrote that the trend is going in the direction to understand LGBT in Japan. But we realized in November 2017 that the world is critical about human rights condition in Japan. The United Nations Human Rights Council released an interim report compiling the **recommendations** by 106 countries for its periodic review, and 218 recommendations for Japan were listed in the report. The list included the issue of "**comfort women**," who were forced to work in World War II military brothels, raised at the request of South and North Korea and China stating, "Japan is not facing the fact of the history."

There were many other recommendations mainly about the discrimination against women, racial, and ethnic minorities as well as discrimination on the ground of sexual orientation. The report stated that Japan's efforts to eliminate the discriminations are not enough. Japan's situation was compared to the **Anti-Discrimination Laws** in the Netherlands. Also, in regard to freedom of the press in Japan, the government was said to intervene as "politically not fair." Moreover, there were many critical opinions concerning the **death penalty** in Japan. Specific recommendation states,

これらの勧告は**人権理事会**が正式採択したので、日本政府は2018年3月までに勧告を受け入れるかどうかの態度表明をしなくてはならなくなった。今のところ外務省は、「韓国は、2015年の**日韓合意**を無視している」という従来からの反論を繰り返した。また、「勧告は、言いたいことを並べただけで、議論を交わして**総論**にまとめたものではない」との認識を示し、判断を保留している。

昨今、セクハラやパワハラが**世間を騒がしている**こともあって、「たしかにひどい状況だ」とは思うが、報道などで知るだけであまり身近にそうした問題に接していない一般人の私としては、「日本だけが、そんなにひどいのか？」、「批判する国の人権事情の方が、もっと深刻じゃないのか！」と思う。ただ、「評判が良くない」という結果が出たのは事実である。とくに上に書いた「女性の活躍」が不十分なことなどは認めて改善する必要がある。

"Temporarily stop the death penalty for now if changing laws is difficult."

As these recommendations by **The United Nations Human Rights Council** were formally adopted, the Japanese government must respond to it regardless of Japans acceptance of the recommendations or not. The Ministry of Foreign Affairs repeated the argument that South Korea is ignoring the **agreement between South Korea and Japan** in 2015. "The preliminary report simply lists remarks, and does not show the **general statement** after discussions," said the ministry, and it is putting the decision on hold.

Lately, the subject of sexual or power harassment is **very much in the air**, and I think the situation of harassment is awful. As I hear these issues on the news, I know they exist for sure. Personally, however, I haven't encountered those issues around me, and honestly, that makes me think "Is Japan's situation so bad? Aren't the situations in other countries criticizing Japan worse than us?" Even so, the result of the report stating that Japan has a bad reputation is a fact. Specifically, we have to admit that the above mentioned "women's active participation in the workplace" is not enough and improve the situation.

だが、国の態度として、国連のこの指摘に対しては**毅然と**、かつ前向きに対処すべきだろう。どんな事実をもとに人権侵害と批判するかをよく調べて、誤解や理解不足があるなら主張して理解させ、改善すべきことがあれば、ひとつずつ取組みを強化するしかないだろう。でも、死刑問題一つをとっても、**一朝一夕に解決する**とは思えない。欧米の制度や価値観にすべて合わせろというのは、国民感情や歴史的経緯、固有の文化を無視する**暴論**である。

Japan's attitude toward the recommendations by the United Nations should be **firm**, and the problems should be dealt with positively. We have to find out on what grounds this criticism of human rights violation is coming from. If there are misunderstandings or lack of understanding, we should insist on the facts and make them understand our real situation. If there are areas that require improvements, we have to work harder to solve the problems one by one. Having said that, I don't think that each problem, such as death penalty, will be **solved overnight**. If the United Nations is saying that Japan should follow the Western system and values, it would be quite an **irrational statement** by ignoring Japan's national sentiment, history, and culture.

移民・難民問題に鈍感すぎる日本

今、EUや米国が抱える深刻な問題は「移民問題」である。どこの国も、当初は「**安い労働力**」と移民を歓迎した。やがて移民が家族を呼び寄せたり、**不法入国**するものや、政治的・宗教的難民の数が急激に増えてくると、それまでのコミュニティとさまざまな**軋轢**が生じるようになった。「仕事を奪われる」、「生活保護費などの**行政サービス**にただ乗りしている」、「自分たちの言語、習慣を変えようとしない」、「権利の要求が一方的過ぎる」……等々。メキシコからの不法移民を追放し、国境に巨大な壁を築くという政策を掲げるトランプ政権の米国は極端な例だが、フランスもドイツも移民や難民を排除・制限する方向に転換した。

移民によって形成された大国・米国にしても、長い時間と数えきれないほどの衝突を繰り返してきた歴史があり、「移民問題」への**免疫や耐性**がどの国よりもあるかと思える。だが、基本的には何も解決しないまま、今も続いているのである。

Japan is too ignorant of immigration and refugee problems

Currently, the big problem for the EU and the U.S. is the immigration issue. Many countries welcomed the immigrants at the beginning as "**cheap labor**." As the immigrants started bringing their families over, and the number of **illegal immigrants** and political and religious refugees rapidly increased, **conflicts** broke out between the immigrants and communities they live in. People in the communities talk about the immigrants as "They take away our work." "They are getting **public assistance** without paying taxes." "They won't change their languages or customs." "They demand too much." And so on. President Trump wants illegal Mexican immigrants out of the U.S., and plans to build giant walls at the borders between the U.S. and Mexico. This is an extreme example, but France and Germany have changed their policies, and they will remove the immigrants and refugees from their countries or limit their entrance.

The United States has been made by immigrants, and it has a long history full of conflicts among immigrants. So, you might think that it would have better **immunity or tolerance** to immigrants than any other country. Fundamentally, however, nothing has been solved and the issue is still there.

移民受け入れに積極的だった“優等生”のスウェーデンも行き過ぎた**移民保護政策**による**財政破綻**の危機を迎えている。スラムが生まれ、移民の暴動事件さえ起きている。現在のペースでは、20年以内にイスラム教徒の移民が国民の半数以上になるとの推計さえある。「スウェーデン・バリュー」と呼ばれる同国の理念は、「男女平等（ジェンダー平等）・人権尊重・個性尊重」だったが、社会の現実とは大きなギャップが生まれている。

こうした欧米に比較すれば、日本はまだ「移民問題」を本気で考えてはいない。**少子高齢化**によって、建設・製造・物流・農業・福祉など、慢性的な「労働力不足」になっている産業では、「移民を受け入れるしかない」との声が出ている。だが、現実的な政策論議としてはレベルが低すぎる。「毎年20万人程度なら良いのでは」とか、「**単純な出稼ぎ移民**は断るが、知識や技術の不足を研修制度の充実で補い、『高度な労働力』にできるなら受け入れよう」などと“**ご都合主義**”的な意見が**まかり通って**いる。今の経済活動の見直しで、サービスレベルが下がることがあっても受け入れられるものもたくさんあるはずだ。コンビニやファストフード店の24時間営業などはその一例だと思う。

Sweden has been actively accepting immigrants, but it is now facing **a fiscal crisis** due to the excessive **immigrant's protection policy**. Some areas are becoming slums, and many riots are happening within immigrant areas. According to an estimation, if immigrants continue to come into Sweden, more than half of its population would become Islam immigrants within 20 years. The national ideology of "Sweden Value" is based on "Gender equality" "Respect for human rights" and "Respect for individuality." But there is a big gap between this value and the reality in this society.

Compared to the Western countries, Japan has not considered the immigration issue seriously yet. Because of the **declining birth rate and an aging population** in Japan, various industries such as construction, manufacturing, logistics, agriculture, and welfare are suffering from chronic labor shortages. People in those industries are expressing their opinion that there is no other way to resolve this but to accept immigrants. But this has not reached the level of realistic policy discussion. Opinions about immigrants that are "**convenient**" for Japanese are **accepted by many** such as "We can accept about 200,000 immigrants every year," "We can't accept **low level migrant workers**, but willingly accept immigrants who can become 'high-level laborers' by setting up good a training system to teach them the knowledge and skills needed." If we

2017年6月現在、**正規の資格**で日本に在住する外国人の総数は約300万人。その8割をアジアが占め、中国（約88万人）、韓国（約54万人）、フィリピン（約27万人）となっている（詳しくは日本政府の統計サイト「e-Stat」）。人口比率にして2.5%にも満たない。この現状のために、「移民問題」をリアルに考えられないのだろう。しかし、世界は流動している。経済破たんや政治不安、軍事衝突、宗教対立、テロなどで、**故国を捨てざるを得ない**人がどこでも大量に発生し、その余波が日本に及ぶ事態もあり得ないことではない。

「日本で暮らすなら日本の文化と市民生活のルールを尊重してね」というような話が通用しない時代に入る。「箸の使い方」をガイジンに説明している場合じゃないのだが……。

review the current economic activities, many businesses should be able to accept immigrants as workers, although the level of service may suffer. Convenience stores or fast-food restaurants that open 24/7 could be a good starting point.

As of June 2017, the total number of foreigners with **proper visas** in Japan was approximately three million. 80% of the immigrants are from Asia such as China (around 880,000 people), Korea (around 540,000 people) and the Philippines (around 270,000 people). (For further details, please refer to the "e-Stat," a statistic web site from the Japanese government.) This represents less than 2.5% of the population ratio in Japan. Because of this status, Japanese people don't think about the immigration issue seriously. But the world is changing. In various places around the world, many people **have no choice but to leave their countries** due to the economic crisis, political uncertainty, military conflict, religious conflict, and terrorism, and those people may come to Japan.

It won't be realistic to ask the immigrants to, "Please respect Japanese culture and the rules as citizens if you live in Japan." Times are changing. It's no use explaining how to use chopsticks to foreigners at this point in time.

構成員が激減する「ヤクザ」の陰で

話がどんどん硬くなりそうなので、日本的話題に趣向を変えよう。いや、別に柔らかい話でもない。

日本では、「あいつはコレだよ」と言って、人差し指で頬を縦に切るサインをすると、「**ヤクザ**」あるいは「暴力団」の意味になる。日本の**闇社会**を支配するギャング勢力として「YAKUZA」は、「日本のマフィア」として海外にも知られた。米国映画『ブラック・レイン』(1989年)や『キル・ビル』(2003年)で知った外国人もいただろう。

どこの国も闇社会は存在するし、いつの時代にも反社会的・暴力的な生き方をする若者はいる。それに彼らと**利害を共有する関係にあった企業家や政治家**もたくさんいる。だが、普通の暮らしをする人にとって、彼らは近寄りたくない存在であるし、話題にすることも控える。日本で「入れ墨」(タトゥー)が**敬遠される**のは、ヤクザのしるしと見られてきた歴史があるからだ。

しかし現在の日本では「ヤクザ」は消えようとしている。1992年3月、市民生活や経済活動を侵食する暴力団の**封じ込め**を目的とする「暴力団対策法」が施行され、警察

Rapidly decreasing number of yakuza (Japanese gangsters)

As the subject is getting more and more serious, I will change it to something Japanese. But even so, it's not a light story.

In Japan, if someone says, "He is this," and makes a gesture of cutting one's cheek with the index finger, it means that he is a **"yakuza" gangster**. Yakuza became globally famous as "Japanese mafia" who own the Japanese **underground world**. Some foreigners might have learned about yakuza through the U.S. movies "Black Rain" (1989) or "Kill Bill" (2003).

In every country, an underground society exists, and at any time, there are anti-social and violent young people. Also, there are many **business entrepreneurs and politicians who have shared interests with them in the past**. But for ordinary people, yakuza is an existence with whom we don't want to have any connections with or talk about them. The reason why tattoos are **avoided** in Japan is that they are historically regarded as the symbol of yakuza.

But nowadays, yakuza is disappearing in Japan. In March 1992, the Anti-Organized Crime Law, which is to **contain** yakuza from bothering ordinary citizens'

が本格的に取り締まりするようになって以来、その勢力は確実に弱まっている。重点的な取締り対象に指定された暴力団の**構成員と準構成員**も減り続け、2016年時点では合計で4万人以下と推定されている。1960年代には15万人以上いたのだから激減ぶりは明らかだ。

またマスコミや市民団体などによる監視も厳しくなり、活動を制約されるだけなく、企業家、政治家、芸能人などは、彼らと接触しているとの噂が立つだけで大きなダメージを受けるようになってきた。それとともに「ヤクザ」をめぐる話題そのものも消えつつある。

飲食店などの営業利権と紛争抑止を名目に要求する上納金を「**みかじめ料**」と呼んだことや、賭博・売春・麻薬などで暮らしを維持することを「しのぎ」と言ったこと、そして冒頭に書いたような指で頬を切るサインなども、現代の若い人には分からなくなっている。言葉の消滅と存在感の消滅は比例するから、悪い傾向ではない。

lives and economic activities, took effect. And since the police started to heavily crackdown on them, its power is steadily weakening. **Members and associate members** of organized crime groups, which have become the target of the focused policing, is continuing to decrease, and its numbers are estimated at less than 40,000 in total in 2016. As there were more than 150,000 yakuza in the 1960s, it is apparent that its number has been dropping drastically.

As mass media and citizens' groups are keeping a close eye on yakuza, they've been forced to limit their activities. Business owners, politicians, and celebrities are now avoiding contacting yakuza because just a rumor of their connections would damage their reputations. Under these circumstances, the topic of yakuza itself is disappearing.

Yakuza demanded **protection rackets called *mikajime-ryō*** for restaurant or other business owners in the name of concession and dispute control. Their source of income, which was gambling, prostitution, and drugs, was called *shinogi*. Nowadays young people will not understand these words, let alone the gesture of cutting one's cheek with an index finger as explained above. Well, it's not a bad thing necessarily because the disappearing of words and the existence that the word represents go hand in hand.

しかし、悪事が人間社会からなくなることはない。覚せい剤取引のように、「ヤクザ」のようなプロに代わって、アマチュアが手を染めるケースは今後も増えるだろう。市民社会への浸透が、より見えにくくなることはこれまで以上に深刻な事態だといえる。ただ、タトゥーは、ヒップホップ好きの若者たちにはオシャレなアイテムになってきた。彼らはヤクザとは**関係ない**。

But crimes will not disappear from our societies. There will be more cases where amateurs deal with drugs instead of professionals like yakuza. In a way, the situations could become more serious than before because yakuza's involvements with society are getting harder to see. On the bright side, tattoos are becoming cool items among young people who love hip-hop music. Those kids, of course, **have no relation** to yakuza.

「右翼」とヤクザの違いは？

日本では、時々大音量で何ごとかをわめいて通行する車を見かける。車には大きなスピーカーと日の丸や**旭日旗**、それに横断幕をつけていることが多い。この車を「**街宣車**」という。つまり街頭に出て自分たちの主張を宣伝するための車という意味であり、通称「右翼」と呼ばれる。市民の**迷惑を顧みない**その喧しさと、暴力的な言葉づかいから、暴力団とかヤクザと間違われるが、彼らは政治的思想集団であり、暴力団の構成員ではない。

かつて1960年～70年代の、世界的にも**左翼勢力**および自由主義者（リベラリスト）が活発に活動した「政治の季節」には、「右翼」は危険な存在だった。演説中の野党党首を壇上で刺殺したのも右翼の少年だったし、新聞社支局に**殴り込み**をかけて2人を死傷させた事件も解決されずに2017年に**時効**を迎えた。主要都市の警察署には、学生運動から派生した過激な左翼勢力を「極左暴力集団」と名付けてその取締り本部を設けたが、看板には、「極右」勢力の取締り本部でもあると書かれていた。

What is the difference between *uyoku* (a right-wing organization) and yakuza?

In Japan, sometimes we hear very loud screams from passing cars. Often, those cars have loud speakers, Japanese flags, **Japanese Rising Sun flags** used on military ships, and banners. These cars are called ***gaisen-sha*** **(propaganda vehicles)** meaning vehicles to promote their argument on the street, and people who are doing it are called *uyoku* (the right wing). *Uyoku* people **don't care about the trouble** they are causing by the loud sounds on the street, and use violent words. So, they are mistaken for yakuza, but they are ideological groups and not members of organized crime groups.

During the 1960s and 1970s, **left-wing powers** and liberalists were very active all over the world, which was known as the "season of politics." During that era, the *uyoku* right-wing was a dangerous existence in Japan. A right-wing boy stabbed an opposition leader to death during his speech on the podium. There was a **raid** on a newspaper branch office killing one and injuring another, which was not solved and the **statute of limitations** on the case ran out in 2017. At the police stations in major cities, regulatory headquarters to control the extreme left power derived from student protests called "extreme left violent group." But the signboards of those headquarters showed that they

この時代の右翼は玉石混淆で、暴力団が資金稼ぎの隠れ蓑として右翼結社を名乗り、個人や企業に献金させるようなこともあった。だが、30～40年の間に、日本の「右翼」も少し変わってきたようだ。左右両翼の**政治的対立**が小規模になってきたことや、**暴力団取締り**が徹底したことなどの理由が考えられる。

現在、右翼が活発に「街宣車」を繰り出すのは、主に、何かしらの反日的言動が見られた国の**出先機関**や、天皇制を批判する勢力、「リベラル」を標榜する一部報道機関などに対してである。右翼の構成員も、一部で「日曜右翼」と揶揄されるように、普段は「**かたぎ**」の仕事についていて、週末や祝日などの休みの時だけ街宣活動に参加する者が増えているという。

このまま右翼の活動が鎮まって町が静かになるのは、市民としては歓迎だ。だが、油断はできない。日中韓の関係は決して良好ではない。また**憲法改正**など左右の対立

were the regulatory headquarters of the "extreme right power" as well.

At that time, the right-wing groups were not simply political ones. Some organized crime groups called themselves the right-wing groups to hide their true identities, and used the groups to collect money from individuals or business owners. But during the last 30 to 40 years, Japanese *uyoku* has changed a little. The reasons for that could be that the scale of **political conflict** between the right and left wing have become smaller, and that the **crackdown of organized crime groups** has been very strict.

Currently, when the *uyoku* right-wing actively drive their propaganda vehicles around, it is limited to appeal to a **local agency** of a country that criticized Japan, forces to criticize the Emperor system or some news media that claims themselves to be liberal. Some members of the right-wing group, who are sometimes called "Sunday right wing" as a joke have "**decent**" day time jobs, and participate in propaganda activities only at weekends and holidays. It is said that the number of those members is increasing.

As a citizen, it would be welcomed if there were less activities by the right-wing and we wouldn't be bothered by their loud noise. But we can't be so sure.

が激化しそうな政治的“火種”もある。「街宣」の趣旨からして、少しでも**目立つ**ことが彼らのアイデンティティなのだから、小さな“火種”が暴動やテロなど、予期せぬ事態になる可能性はあるのだ。

おまけの話。ネット万能時代になって登場したニューフェイスの「右翼」がいる。**匿名で**コメントを書き込む**「掲示板」サイト**の中で、過激な右翼的コメントを書き込む連中のことで「ネトウヨ＝ネット内の右翼」と呼ばれる。リアルな社会つまり駅前などで演説したり、街宣車でデモするような行動はしないが、攻撃対象を見つけるとピラニアのように食いついて、掲示板で一斉に批判したり、プライベートな情報も調べて公開してしまうから、厄介な存在である。

The relationship among Japan, China, and South Korea is not so great now. And the **amendment to the constitution** could become a political "trigger" to intensify the clash between the right and left-wing groups. The purpose of the "propaganda vehicles" is to **draw attention**, and that is the identity of the right-wing groups. So just a small "trigger" might cause unexpected situations like riots or terrorism.

There is more about the right-wing. In this internet age, a new face of the right-wing has appeared. On **bulletin board websites** where users comment **anonymously**, some people write extremely right-wing comments. They are called "*neto-uyo* ('*neto*' is short for 'internet', and '*uyo*' is '*uyoku*')." They don't act in the real world; they don't make speeches in front of the train stations, they don't drive propaganda vehicles around or anything like that. But once they find a target on the internet, they snap at it like a piranha, and they criticize the target on the bulletin board all together, or worse, find out the target's private information and release it on the net. They are very annoying indeed.

偏在するネット・カメラが時代を変える

20年ほど前、コンピュータ科学の分野で「ユビキタス(ubiquitous)」という言葉が流行した。日本語で訳せば「どこにでもある＝偏在する」の意味になるが、この時の意味は、インターネットによって、どこでもコンピュータやICデバイスが使えるということだった。それが、今はスマートフォンやセンサー群と繋がるIoT(Internet of things：モノのインターネット)時代に入った。中でも時代を大きく変えているデバイスが、**ネットにも繋がったカメラ**である。

街中にも、店内にも、工場にも監視カメラ(surveillance camera)が付いている。車のダッシュボードにもある。個人(少なくともほとんどの成人)のスマートフォンもほとんどが**高性能のカメラ内蔵**タイプである。加えて、YouTubeやSNS(Facebook、Instagramなど)の利用者によって、それらの画像は、瞬時に、世界中に配信されてしまう。配信のレビュー数に応じて報酬を設けているサイトもあるから、この傾向にますます**拍車がかかる**。

先日の事件では、高速道路で前の車に異常接近して「煽り立てる」ドライバーが摘発された。容疑者は、車を追い立てたあげく、前に回って車を停めさせ暴力をふるって去った。ひと昔前だったら、このような被害を受けたこ

Ubiquitous internet cameras change the world

About twenty years ago, “ubiquitous” was the buzzword in the computer science field. The original meaning of“ubiquitous” is, “seeming to be everywhere.” But at that time, it meant that people can use computers or IC devices anywhere thanks to the internet. But now, we are in the era of the IoT (Internet of things) where various things are connected via smartphone or censor group. The device that is especially changing the world is **cameras connected to the Internet**.

Around the streets, inside shops and factories, surveillance cameras are everywhere. They are installed on the dashboard in a car. Most of the smart phones that everyone (well, most of the adults) have been equipped with **built-in high-performance cameras**. The pictures taken using those cameras are uploaded to YouTube or SNS (Facebook, Instagram and so on), and they are distributed in the world instantly. As some websites pay money according to the reviewer’s number for the distribution, this trend is being **spurred** on more and more.

At an accident that happened recently, a man drove too close to a car in front of him on the expressway, and was arrested on suspicion of causing an accident. The suspect allegedly chased the victims’ car, stopped

とを立証することは困難だった。悔しいままに沈黙することを「**泣き寝入り**」という。しかし今回は被害者の車に搭載された「ダッシュ・カム（dash cam：dashboard camera）が、一部始終を記録していたので、それが**証拠**となり「泣き寝入り」せずにすんだのである。

記録された画像・動画が、雄弁な証拠として**犯罪抑止**に繋がることは良いことである。しかし、**盗撮**やプライバシーを侵害したり、映画館やコンサート会場で無断録画・録音するようなマイナス面も増えている。単にスマホを見ているだけでも、シチュエーションしだいでは、犯罪者とみなされるかもしれないのだ。**法的整備**がテクノロジーと利用形態の進化に追いつけないまま、ガジェットの大好きな日本人は、全員、**変質者**かとみなされる。

便利すぎる文明の道具を手にした人類は、もう、後戻りできないのだ。

it by stopping his car in front of the victims' vehicle, assaulted one of the victims, and left. In the past, it was very difficult for a victim to prove such a case. In Japanese, when someone is compelled to bear silently, we say "***naki neiri* (cry oneself to sleep)**." But this time, the whole thing was recorded by the dashboard camera on the victims' car, and it was used as a **proof**. The victims didn't have to "cry themselves to sleep" in this case.

It is a good thing that the recorded pictures and videos are used as eloquent evidence, and serves as a **crime deterrent**. However, negative effects are increasing such as **nonconsensual photos** and invasions of privacy as well, or recordings without permission at movie theaters or music concerts. By just looking at a smart phone, you could be regarded as a criminal depending on the situation. The **development of laws** is not catching up with the technologies and evolution of the utilization form of technologies. So, it could be possible that all Japanese might be regarded as **perverts** because we love cool tech gadgets.

Humankind got the tools of civilization, which is too useful, in its hands, and there is no going back any more.

宗教紛争に無知で「ノーテンキ」な日本

日本のマスコミで大活躍している人気の評論家・池上彰氏が、2013年の日本経済新聞のコラムにこんなことを書いていた。

「中東のサウジアラビアなどに入国するときの**入国書類**を書く際は、名前を書き、次に自分の宗教を書く欄があります。かつて日本の若者が、『そんなものないや』と『none（なし）』と書いたのです。そうしたら、**入国審査**で身柄を拘束され、**国外追放**になったそうです。現地の彼らにしてみると、『神様を信じていないようなヤツは、神を恐れぬ人物だから、どんな恐ろしいことをするか分からない。テロリストじゃないか。そんな危険人物をわが国に入れるわけにはいかない』と判断したようなのです」

このエピソードは伝聞として書かれているので、本当かどうかはわからない。だが、似たような話はしばしば聞く。海外に長期滞在の経験がある友人は、「外国人との付き合いが深くなると宗教の話題が出る。そして『お前の宗教は？』と聞かれた時、『無宗教だ』と答えたら、とたんに表情が変わって、『**無神論者**か……』と言われた。以来、『仏教徒』とか『神道だ』と言ってごまかして、その場をやり過ごすようにしている」と話してくれた。

Japan is ignorant and "carefree" about religious conflicts

Akira Ikegami, a very popular critic who has been doing a wonderful job in mass media in Japan, wrote a column on the Nihon Keizai Shimbun in 2013 as below:

"When you fill out an **immigration card** when you enter Middle Eastern countries such as Saudi Arabia, the first column listed on the document is the name, and the next one is religion. One time, a Japanese young person wrote 'None' in the column because he didn't have any specific religions that he believed in. He was detained at the **immigration** and **deported**. It looks that the immigration officers judged that 'He doesn't believe in God nor is afraid of God. We don't know what kind of awful thing such a person might do. He could be a terrorist, and we can't let the dangerous person come into our country.'"

Ikegami wrote this episode as something he heard about, so we don't know if this happened or not. But I often hear similar stories. A friend of mine has stayed in foreign countries for a long time, and he said, "If you develop close relationships with foreigners, they will ask you about your religion. One time, I replied to the question that I believed in no religion. My friend was so shocked and told me, 'You are an **atheist**…' Since

日本人の多くは、神様に**初詣**して、バレンタインにチョコレートをもらい、ハロウィンで騒ぎ、クリスマスにはフライド・チキンを食べ、葬儀はお寺で……という**無節操**な（?）宗教生活をしている。それは「無神論」というより「多神教的」「汎神論的」と呼ぶしかない。**絶対的な神への信仰**を生きる支えとする人たちからみたら、かなり風変わりな文明に思われるのも止むを得ない。

米国の国際政治学者であるサミュエル・ハンチントンは1996年に『文明の衝突』(The Clash of Civilization and Remaking of World Order) という分厚い本を書いた。持つだけでも重たくて、繰り返される主張に飽きて、眠くなる本であった。もう中身もほとんど忘れてしまったが、たしかこんなことが書かれていたと思う。

「**東西冷戦構造**が消滅した世界は、政治やイデオロギーではなく**文明**によって分断されるようになった。世界にはおよそ８つの文明があり、その境目（断層線：Fault Line) で紛争が生じるようになった」

then, I've decided to say that I'm a Buddhist or believer in Shintoism, although I'm not actually. But it's better that way."

Many Japanese **visit shrines or temples on New Year's Day**, get chocolates on Valentine's Day, enjoy Halloween, eat fried chicken on Christmas Eve, and have funerals at temples. We are so **inconsistent** when it comes to religion. Our excuse is that we are "polytheistic" or "pantheistic" rather than "atheistic." From the standpoint of the people who have **strong faith in one god**, our religious culture would look very unusual, and I wouldn't blame them.

Samuel Huntington, an American international political scientist, wrote a thick book called "The Clash of Civilizations and the Remaking of World Order" in 1996. It was so heavy just to hold. I got bored with his repetitive opinion, and it made me sleepy. I don't remember much of it, but I remember something from the book as follows:

"After the end of the **Cold War structure**, the world was divided, not by politics or ideology, but by **civilization**. There are about eight civilizations in the world, and clashes of civilizations are most likely along the 'fault lines' of civilizations."

彼の言う「文明」がいまひとつ曖昧なのだが、その核を宗教と見ているのは確かで、西欧対非西欧の対立、とりわけ西欧文明とイスラム文明の対立は激化し、**和解はない**と断定していたのが印象的だった。その後に起きた2001年の米国同時多発テロやアフガン、イランなどの紛争を予言したとも評価された。非西洋文明の中には、**儒教**をベースにした中華文明やヒンズー教、イスラム教などが含まれるのだが、日本は固有で、どれにも属さないとしていた。たしかに、少数派の文明（宗教）であることは当たっているが、彼は日本の将来について、変な予言を付け加えた。「米国の影響を離れて中国にすり寄る」というのだが、これはまったく的中していない。だから、今、この本を読み直す人も少ないのだろう。

しかし、日本の歴史の中には、**宗教的対立や紛争**がなかったわけではない。古代には仏教を受け入れるか否かの争いがあったし、**戦国時代**には、「一向宗」が一国を支配したこともあったし、同じ仏教内でも「法華宗」と「浄土宗・一向宗」の相互襲撃事件もあった。1995年には「オウム真理教」の地下鉄サリン事件もあった。それでも現代の日本人は、世界各地で起きている宗教対立の知識も関心も低いままである。これは少しまずいのではないだろ

group. Still, present-day Japanese have little knowledge of, and don't have much interest in religious conflicts happening around the world. We should be better than that. Few Japanese are aware that, within Islam, the majority sect in Saudi Arabia is Sunni Muslims, and in Iran, Shiite Muslims. (In Japan, the knowledge or amount of information about the Middle East is **overwhelmingly** limited!).

Even if the Japanese people can't change their "**pantheistic religious lives**," they have to know, as common sense, that the cause of **minority genocides** is deep-rooted religious conflicts. If they don't have that kind of common sense, the world would think of us as "**carefree**" people who know nothing about the movement of the world.

「菊のカーテン」が再び揺れる時

先にChapter 2で、天皇の「生前退位」が**例外的措置**で確定した話を書いた。そこで天皇や皇室を巡る報道には「菊のカーテン」があることや、天皇即位の儀礼である「大嘗祭」の式典が公開されることはないだろうと書いた。「菊のカーテン」と言う言葉は、1946年に英国のチャーチルが、東西冷戦の状態を指して、「バルト海のステッティンからアドリア海のトリエステにいたるまで“鉄のカーテン”が大陸を横切って降ろされている」と演説した「**鉄のカーテン**」をもじったものだ。

欧州にもアジア、中東にも**立憲王政**の国はたくさんあるが、日本のように長い歴史を持つ家系の天皇を抱く国はない。幕府体制を覆して生まれた明治政府は、**天皇を神格化して権威づける**ことに熱心だった。戦争を遂行した勢力も、この権威を大いに利用した。しかし第二次大戦終結の翌年1月（1946年)、天皇はみずから「人間宣言」を行って、新憲法下で**象徴的存在**であることを明確にした。天皇や皇族たちも常に「よりオープンで身近な皇室でありたい」と口にするのだが、「菊のカーテン」の紐を握っているのは所轄官庁である**宮内庁**であり、慎重な姿勢をなかなか崩さない。少なくとも、英国など他の立憲君主国のような水準までオープンにはなっていない。だが、このカーテンがさらに大きく揺さぶられる事態が何十年後かには再びやってくる。

When the "Chrysanthemum curtain" moves again

Previously in Chapter 2, I wrote that Emperor's abdication has been decided as an **exceptional measure**. I mentioned the existence of the "Chrysanthemum curtain," and *daijō-sai* ceremony, a ceremony of the emperor's enthronement, which won't be seen by the public. The name "Chrysanthemum curtain" was borrowed from the expression Winston Churchill used in his 1946 speech about the Cold War; "From Stettin in the Baltic to Trieste in the Adriatic, an '**iron curtain**' has descended across the Continent."

In Europe, Asia, and the Middle East, many countries have **constitutional monarchies**, but none of them have the one that has a long history of family line like Japan's Emperor does. The Meiji government was born after overthrowing the Tokugawa shogunate, and it was eager to **deify the emperor to authorize itself**. The power that carried out the war greatly used the Emperor's authorization. After World War II, the Emperor Shōwa (Hirohito) issued the "Human Declaration" in January 1946, and made it clear that he is the **symbol of the state** under the new Constitution. Emperor Akihito and other members of the imperial family often say, "The Imperial Household should be more open and closer to the people." However, the

現在の皇太子（徳仁：なるひと）が新しい天皇に即位するのは2019年元旦とされている。しかし、その子供は女性で**内親王**（敬宮愛子：としのみやあいこ）である。現在の憲法2条には、「皇位は、世襲のものであって、国会の議決した**皇室典範**の定めるところにより、これを継承する。」とある。その「皇室典範」第1条には、「皇位は、皇統に属する**男系**の男子が、これを継承する。」と記されているから、内親王は皇位継承順位からははずされる。1位は現皇太子、2位は5歳違いの弟・秋篠宮文仁（あきしののみやふみひと）親王、3位はその長男である悠仁（ひさひと）親王となっている。しかし、何十年か後になれば、「憲法を改正して、女性が天皇になっても良いではないか」という議論は必ず高まるだろう。過去には何人も女性天皇は存在したからだ。

Imperial Household Agency, which is in charge of the imperial household, is holding the tassel of the "Chrysanthemum curtain," and it maintains a cautious stance to this matter. At least, the Japanese Imperial Family's openness hasn't reached the same level as other constitutional monarchies such as the U.K. But, within a few decades, the situation where this curtain would be shaken hard would surely happen in Japan.

The enthronement date of Crown Prince Naruhito is scheduled on New Year's Day in 2019. But he only has a daughter, **Princess** Aiko (Toshinomiya Aiko). Article 2 of the Constitution of Japan reads, "The Imperial Throne shall be dynastic and succeeded to in accordance with the **Imperial House Law** passed by the Diet." In Article 1 of the Imperial House Law, it is written as follows: "The Imperial Throne shall be succeeded by a male offspring in the **male line** belonging to the Imperial Lineage." So, Princess Aiko will not be included in the line of succession to the Japanese throne. First in line is Crown Prince Naruhito, second Prince Akishino (Akishino-no-miya Fumihito) five years younger than his brother, and the third Prince Hisahito of Akishino, his son. In several decades from now, there will be active discussions about changing the Japanese Constitution so that a princess can become an emperor. In fact, there were several female emperors in the history of Japan.

この「女系天皇問題」も重要だが、個人的に「菊のカーテン」を開きたいのは、「**御陵**問題」だ。日本各地には、歴代天皇・皇族らが葬られた御陵が「**古墳**」として存在する。しかし、これを学術目的で**発掘調査**することが許されていない。そのために、古墳の主を科学的に特定することも進まず、日本の古代史が謎のままだ。まずは、こちらのカーテンを開けて欲しい。

I know this "female emperor matter" is important, but personally, I'd like to open the "Chrysanthemum curtain" for the "**Imperial mausoleum** problem." There are several Imperial mausoleums, where the past emperors and imperial families were buried, that exist as "**ancient tombs**" in various places in Japan. But conducting **excavations** of those tombs for academic research is not permitted. Because of that, we can't scientifically specify who are buried in the tombs, and our ancient history remains a mystery. This is the "curtain" that has to be opened.

CHAPTER

5

タブーと向き合うための5つのキーワード

Five keywords to face taboos

動物は生まれついて聖なるものではないし、愛を最優先しないし、真理や善を尊ぶものではない。放っておけば欲望のままに動いてしまい、争い、殺し合いさえする。社会生活する動物である人間は、**共同体**を維持し、違う集団との共存を図るために、タブーや戒律、ルールを作ってきたのかもしれない。しかし、現代社会は、**見えざるタブー**が増殖し、ルールによって、より細かく規制されるようになってきた。それが有用な活力まで削ぐことになっているような危機感がある。タブーやルールに自縛されずに、日本人が輝くために必要と思われることを５つのキーワードにまとめてみた。

Animals are not sacred by nature. They don't think love is the most important thing, and they don't respect the truth or good. If left alone, they act as they want, fight or even kill each other. Human beings are social animals. Taboos, commandments, and rules might have been made to keep the **communities** and live together with other groups. In contemporary society, however, there are more **invisible rules**, and everything is getting regulated in detail by those rules. I have a sense of crisis that those invisible taboos or rules might be contributing to the loss of good vitality within society. I've compiled following five keywords in order for Japanese to be free from taboos and rules, and can live happily.

キーワード1● 現実的視点

「ニッポン、いいね！」に距離を置く

訪日外国人たちが日本の景観や和食や、日本人の**規律**や“おもてなし”を賛美するTV番組（「ニッポン、いいね！（thumbs-up）」）やネットブログがたくさん見受けられるようになった。まるでコーラスのようだ。実際、観光客は年々急増しているし、観光地としての評価も高まっている。何であれ、他者から賞賛されれば誰だってうれしくなる。他者が**再発見**してくれる日本の美点に、自分たちも感動したりする。「自分たちの国と文化は、なかなか良いらしい」と再認識する。しかし、**「いいね！」の声を鵜呑みにする**のはちょっと危うい。日本の諺でいうのなら「**井の中の蛙**」状態になってしまう危険性がある。日本を持ち上げる評価なんて、全然客観的ではないし、永続するものではない。「いいね！」の評価も、**一部の材料を多重に引用し**、編集を加えたものである。隠されるか削除された「良くない！（thumbs-down）」の声も同量あると考えるのがリアリスティックな態度だろう。

しかし、現在の「いいね！」コーラスの中で、「良くない！」と声を上げることはタブー視される。「少なくとも

Keyword 1 ● **Be realistic**

Doubt "Nippon, Cool!" comments

"Nippon *Iine*! (Thumbs up Japan!)" was a TV program where foreign visitors praise beautiful Japanese scenery, meals, **disciplines**, and *omotenashi* (hospitality). And many other blogs with similar content have been seen on the Internet recently. It's almost like a chorus. In fact, the number of tourists has been rapidly increasing every year, and Japan's reputation as a tourist destination is going up. Whatever it is, it is nice to be praised by other people. Foreign visitors help us **rediscover** the beauty of Japan. We can appreciate that our country and culture is not so bad. But to **accept those "Thumbs up!" without questioning** would be too naïve. As a Japanese proverb says, "**The frog in the well knows nothing of the great ocean**." It describes a person who is ignorant of the real world, and we might become that "frog" if we simply believe the praise by foreigners. The good reputation of Japan is not objective at all, it won't continue forever. Those "Thumbs up!" are based on **very limited materials, and they are quoted repeatedly** with some editing. It would be realistic to think that there would be the same numbers of hidden or deleted "Thumbs down!" as "Thumbs up!"

But it is regarded as a taboo to say, "Thumbs down!" when everybody else is saying "Thumbs up!" There is

2020年の東京五輪までは、このブームが続いてほしい」と願う**社会の圧力**がある。「道路にはゴミひとつ落ちていなくて清潔」、「自動販売機が普及していて便利」、「**和食**が多彩でヘルシーで見た目も美しい」、「誰もが優しく親切に接してくれる」……こんな声は、現実の半面しかみていないか、お世辞（リップサービス）の類である。ゴミが散らかった汚い場所はヤマほどあるし、自販機なんて景観上も邪魔でしかない。懐石料理は味も量ももの足りないし、牛肉やマグロ（トロ）やサーモンの脂肪を有難がるのは**味覚障害**に近い。海外で急増しているまがい物の和食や奇妙な寿司についても、何も言えない。日本だって各国の料理を現地化してきた歴史がある。人々の優しさや丁寧さは事実としても、短期的・表面的な接触ではないのか？**本音は曖昧な微笑の陰に隠す**ことも多い。

日本人が**目を向ける**べき分野は他にある。たとえば歴史的建造物や伝統工芸、産業や暮らしの末端を支えてきた**職人**にしても、**維持や継承**がままならないところまで来ていることだ。そろそろ、「いいね！」のコーラスには少し距離を置いて、本当に価値あるものを冷静に見極め、

a **social pressure** that we want this boom to continue at least until 2020 Tokyo Olympics and Paralympics. "There is no garbage on the road, and it is very clean." "There are many vending machines around, and it is convenient." "**Japanese cuisine** has many varieties, and it is healthy and beautiful as well." "Everybody is very kind." These are the voices either half true or lip service. In reality, there are many places with a lot of garbage, and vending machines are ugly to look at. *Kaiseki-ryōri*, a traditional Japanese meal brought in courses, lacks in taste and volume. People who love the fatty part of beef, tuna (*toro*), and salmon must have a **taste disorder** or something. We can't complain about strange Japanese dishes and sushi that are rapidly gaining popularities overseas. But Japan has a history of adopting dishes from all over the world as well. Japanese people might be gentle or polite. But that kind of impression might be coming from only short and brief contact with Japanese. It would be difficult for foreigners to understand what Japanese really think because we tend to **hide our true feelings behind quiet smiles**.

What Japanese should really **pay attention** to is in different fields. For example, we have come to the point where only a few **craftsmen** exist, and it is becoming very difficult to **maintain or inherit** historic structures, traditional handicrafts, and industries. We have to

それらの維持や継承に努力し支援することが重要ではないだろうか？

distance ourselves from the "Thumbs up!" chorus. It is important to see things that are really valuable, and try to keep or inherit them, or help people who are making those efforts.

キーワード2● 闘う気構え

隣人は"地獄の使者"かもしれない

YouTubeで再生回数が多い海外投稿に、「Neighbors from Hell」というカテゴリーがある。直訳すれば「地獄から来た隣人」である。勝手にフェンスを動かす、ゴミを投げ込む、玄関前に駐車する、四六時中クレームをつける、浴室に向けてビデオカメラを向けている、ブルドーザで家を破壊する……等々、隣人たちのありとあらゆる**迷惑行為**が投稿されている。いくら抗議されても謝らず、言動も改めず、おとなしくしていれば「黙認」とみなし、自分の**既得権**と見なす。抗議すればカサにかかって反撃するのだから手に負えない。

日本でも隣人問題として、「ゴミ屋敷住人」や、「騒音ババア」などが話題になる。昔のように近隣住民の**共同体意識**が強ければ、団結してこの連中を非難したり、追放したりもできたかもしれないが、今は「個」の時代だとして互いに干渉することを避ける。頼みとする行政や警察も「**民事不介入**」で腰が引けているから、簡単には片付かない。相手が日本人ならともかく、価値観や習慣の異なる外国人となればなおさらだ。キリストは「汝の隣人を愛せよ」

Keyword 2 ● **Fighting spirit**

Your neighbor could be a "messenger from hell"

A category called "Neighbors from Hell" on YouTube receives a lot of views.

The "Neighbors from Hell" videos include all sorts of **annoying activities** such as moving fences without asking the neighbor, throwing garbage into a neighbor's yard, parking a car in front of a neighbor's house, complaining about everything all the time, aiming a video camera to a neighbor's bathroom, destroying a neighbor's house by a bulldozer, and on and on.

They don't apologize or change their behavior despite the repeated complaints from the neighbors. If the neighbors don't say anything, they think that their actions are "OK" and regard it as an "**acquired right**." If the neighbors challenge them, they fight back, and there is nothing the neighbors can do to stop them.

Similarly, in Japan, we have the neighbors from hell such as "people who live in a house full of garbage and junk" or "noisy old women." If **community identities** are strong as they used to be, people in the community could have criticized the neighbors from hell or made them move. But now, as we are living in the age of respect the "individuality," we avoid interfering with other people's lives. We can't rely on the government

と「**隣人愛**（アガペー）」の大切さを説いたが、相手が「価値観が真逆＝地獄からの使者」だとなれば話は別。これはもう、戦って撃滅するしかないことになる。

しかし、多くの日本人は、他人とくに見知った隣人と諍いを起こすことを極端に敬遠する。諍いそのものをタブー視する。法にのっとっての訴訟ごとにも不慣れである。何しろ古代以来、「**和をもって貴しとなす**」という言葉が大好きで、ビジネスなどの契約書でも、**互いの利害が相反する場合の条項**を詳しく想定することもなく、末尾に「問題が起きた場合は、双方が誠意をもって話し合うこと」と書いてすませてしまう。欧米企業と交わす契約書の分厚さとはまるで別物だ。日本人の「諍い嫌い」な気質が、もう通用しない時代になっていることに気づくべきだろう。

冒頭のYouTube投稿で目につくのは、諍いあう双方が「My Property（俺んちの財産だ）」と声高に言い合ってい

or police because of their "**nonintervention of civil cases**" policy. So, the resolution of this matter isn't so simple. If the neighbors from hell are Japanese, the thing might be rather simple. But if they are foreigners with different values and customs, things could get more complicated. Jesus Christ taught us to "love your neighbor as yourself" and the importance of the "**neighborly love** (agape)." It's a different story, however, when the neighbors from hell have totally opposite values. It's time to fight.

Most Japanese hate to fight, especially against somebody you know well such as the neighbors. Fighting itself is regarded as a taboo in Japan. We are not used to suing other people under the law as well. From ancient times, Japanese love the expression that says, "**Cherish the harmony among people**." Even in a business contract, we don't set up a **specific article for potential conflicts of interest**, but instead simply state "Any matter not stipulated in this Agreement shall be resolved upon mutual consultation between both parties." It is totally different from the thick contracts made by Western companies. But Japanese should realize that we are living in the era when our characters to hate dispute will no longer be accepted.

In the YouTube videos mentioned before, the most impressive thing is that the people in dispute

る姿だ。そう、「自分の財産や権利が侵されている」ときっちり主張することが基本なのだ。「そのうち自分の主張の非を認めて、言動を改めてくれるだろう」と言っていたら、財産や権利への侵略は**底なし**になり、こちらが逃げ出す羽目になる。ここで、「隣人」を「隣国」と置き換えて考えてみるのは、少し勇気が必要かもしれないが、どこの国も隣国との歴史的関係は**円満ではない**のだから気にする必要はない。中国も韓国も空間的には「自国領土だ」と主張し、時間的には「正しい歴史認識を」と声を上げているではないか。諍いはもう向こうから仕掛けられている。

戦う姿勢を持つといっても、物理的な暴力ではなく、しかるべき**法的裏付け**と証拠を揃え、訴訟などに持ち込むという手段である。国と国の問題なら**国際裁判所**に証拠を積み上げれば良い。そして、**ことの是と非**を明らかにし、主張すべきことは必ず声に出すべき時が来ている。

scream, "It's my property!" to each other. Yes, it is the fundamental basic to clearly claim that one's own property or rights are invaded. If you think that your neighbor would eventually admit his wrong doing and change his attitude, you are wrong. The neighbor's invasion to your wealth and rights would become **unstoppable**, and eventually you would be forced to leave. I have to be rather brave to say this, but we could use the word "neighbor country" instead of "neighbor" in my previous sentence. Well, every country has **rather bumpy** historical relationships with the neighboring country, so I wouldn't have to worry too much. Regarding the territorial disputes that are going on between Japan and neighboring countries, both China and South Korea claim their ownership of the properties, and they are asking Japan to "recognize the history correctly." It was them who started the disputes.

What I meant by "fight" is not physical acts of violence but to start lawsuits against them, and that should be **supported by proper laws** and evidence. If the dispute is between two countries, we can submit the evidence to the **International Court of Justice**. The time has come for Japanese to make clear **what is right and what is wrong**, and appeal what should be appealed.

何でも「道」にするのはやめて

「柔道」、「剣道」、「弓道」、「合気道」、「空手道」……**日本発祥**の武術、格闘技（マーシャル・アーツ）は、世界中に道場が生まれていて、大変な人気がある。ここで気づいただろうか？　そのほとんどが「道」という文字がついている。そう、その歩いたり走ったりする「road」である。

武術だけではない、生け花のことは「華道」というし、お茶（抹茶）を立てる作法は「茶道」であり、香の種類をかぎ分ける「香道」というものもある。日本人は、訓練（トレーニング）が必要なことならなんでも「道」にしたがる傾向がある。**禅の影響**だという人もいるが、それだけではないだろう。「まじめに努力を続ける」のが好きな日本人らしい価値観だ。

実利的・実用的な観点からいえば、武術なら「戦って勝ちを得れば良い」だけのことであり、花は美しくアレンジされればそれで良く、お茶も美味しければそれで良いはずだ。しかし、「道」がつく修行や稽古事では、「結果は問題ではない」と考える。「終わりのない道を歩むように、ゴールのない、**自己研鑽**を続ける姿勢」を高く評価する。

Say goodbye to *dō* (the way)

Martial arts such as Jūdō (柔道), Kendō (剣道), Kyūdō (弓道), Aikidō (合気道), and Karatedō (空手道) were **born in Japan**. They are very popular, and there are many *dōjō* training schools all over the world now. As you might have noticed, most of the names of Japanese martial arts have a Chinese character "道 (*dō*)" in them. This character means "road," and it is the same character as a physical ordinary road for walking or running.

This "road" is not limited to martial arts. Flower arrangement is *kadō* (華道), manners in Japanese tea ceremony is *sadō* (茶道), and traditional incense-smelling ceremony is *kōdō* (香道). Japanese tend to make everything into *dō* that requires training. Some say this is coming from the **influence of Zen**, but I think there is more to it. It is the Japanese value of liking to keep practicing achieving one's goal.

From the **practical standpoint**, only winning should matter in martial arts, only beautifully arranged flowers should matter in flower arrangement, and only tasty tea should matter at a tea ceremony. But in martial arts and hobbies that have *dō* in their names, it is considered that "the results don't matter." It is highly respected to keep

このことが、異文化の人には不思議であるし不合理と感じる要因にもなっている。

しかしこれが、武術のように国際的なスポーツになってしまうと、この「道」の精神と、勝負の**明確な基準**を求めるニーズとが摩擦を起こしかねない。オリンピックなどで「柔道」がポイント制になったことから、「勝つための柔道、**ポイント稼ぎのためのテクニック**」が主流になって、技の美しさやフェアな精神性が損なわれたと嘆く日本の柔道関係者は多い。でも、どんなに崇高な精神と立派なフェアプレイを見せても、勝てないのでは評価されなくなる。

おそらく、これらの**稽古事**も、生まれた当初には、やはり結果や**実利的な効用**を重視したはずだ。それが、上手になるほど結果や効用はもはや当然のこととみなして、それ以上の価値として精神性や立ち居振る舞いの所作、相手への敬意などを重視することになったのだと思われる。だが、精神性や所作の優雅さ、自分の技に対する謙虚さなどには明確なゴールも**指標**もない。そこで「道」という字がついたのだ。

on **improving one's skills** like walking on an endless road with no goals. This kind of attitude looks very strange and irrational for foreigners.

When it comes to martial arts, as they have become international sports, this spirit of *dō* and the needs for a **clear standard** of winning and losing might have conflict. Ever since Judo took up a point system at the Olympic games, many Japanese Judo people lament and say, "The mainstream of Jūdō now is Jūdō for winning, and only the **techniques to earn points** matter." They also say that the beauty of Jūdō techniques and fair spirit are lost. At the end of the day, however, even if you can show the high spirit and fair play, you would be nobody if you can't win.

I would assume that when the **lessons** of martial arts and other forms of art such as flower arrangement originally started, the results and **practical benefits** must have been important. As people's skills improved, the results or practical benefits would be considered as a matter of course, and higher values such as spirituality, action manners, and respect to the others must have become more important. As there was no clear goal or **target** in the spirituality, elegant manners, and humbleness for one's own skills, the character "道" must have been added to the names of martial arts and other forms of art.

近年では、日本文化のこうした側面を魅力的に感じる外国人も増えているようだが、まだまだ**少数派**であるし、その価値は一般の人にわかりにくい。武術にしても茶道にしても、やはり実利や結果がすべてなのである。明快な基準を持った判定には説得力がある。その上で精神性や美しさも伴えば理想的だ。この**順序を逆転**させて、「道」にこだわり過ぎたら結局は愛好者を失うことになる。あえて言おう。**世界に通用しない**「道」の精神は忘れて、実利や結果の出せる工夫をもっとすべきだ、と。

Recently, the number of foreigners, who are attracted to this kind of aspect of Japanese culture, has been increasing, but they are still **minorities**. The value of "道" is hard to understand for ordinary people. Even for martial arts or tea ceremonies, the result and practicality is everything. Judgments based on a clear standard are persuasive. If the spirituality and beauty are added to the judgments, that would be idealistic. If this **order is reversed** and *dō* is given too much emphasis, we might lose the people who are interested in martial or other forms of arts in the end. I would rather say this. Forget the *dō* spirit that **doesn't work in the world**, and put more effort on results and practicalities.

キーワード4● 個性と独立心

「自分らしさ」を愉しみ尊重する社会

私が若かった頃の恥ずかしい体験。ある企業の社長の希望で、売れっ子の著名な評論家と食事をする機会を設けた。社長は仕事では**辣腕家**で知られ、リーダーシップもある立派な人なのだが、この時は、評論家との初対面に緊張したらしく、いつもの気迫がなかった。

食事前、ウェイターに「何か飲み物を？」と聞かれ、評論家は「ワシはいつもカンパリのソーダ割りやけど、あんたらどうしますか？」と質問をこちらに向けた。すると社長は「私もそれで」、同席した秘書も「同じもので」と答え、**末席**の私もつい「同じく」と答えてしまった。評論家は、「なんでワシに合わせんねん。あんたら会社の人は昼酒はせんでしょうに。カンパリもふだんは呑まへんとちゃいますか？」と呆れ、社長以下、自分も赤面した。

しかし対談は、これがきっかけになって、評論家はお得意の話題、「そもそも日本人は**同調したがる**ねん。……」で盛り上がったのだから、恥は帳消しだった。それにしても、なんでカンパリ・ソーダなんか頼んでしまったのだろう。

Society to respect "personality"

I will confess my embarrassing experience when I was young. The president of a company asked me to set up a lunch meeting with a famous critique. The president is known to be an **avid business person** and has good leadership skills. But that time, he must have been very nervous to meet with the critique for the first time, and he wasn't as powerful as usual.

Before the lunch, a waiter asked us about the drinks. The critique said, "I'll have my usual Campari and soda," and asked us, "What would you guys like to have?" The president replied, "I'll have the same," and his secretary said, "Me, too," then I, seating at the **seat of least honor**, said, "Me, too," without thinking. The critique was surprised and asked us, "Why did you order the same thing as mine? I don't think you usually drink alcohol at lunch, do you? And I would assume you don't normally drink Campari, do you?" The president, his secretary and I all blushed in shame.

Surprisingly, the meeting went very well because the Campari "incident" lead to the critique's favorite topic, which is "Why Japanese **agree with other people so easily**?" After all, our shame turned into a good subject of conversation. Looking back, I still don't know why I

よく言えば**協調的**で規律を守る、他人の振る舞いを見て、なるべくそれに合わせようとする。これが良い面に出れば、震災時の給水に並んだり、公共輸送機関に**整列乗車**することになる。例の「日本人すごい！」コーラスが頻出する光景である。しかし、悪い面に出ると、上に書いた「カンパリ・ソーダ」風になってしまう。**無批判に**他人と横並びして安心する。「個」が消えて集団の中に埋没・同調してしまうことになる。

このことに気づいていた日本の教育界では、長い間「個性を伸ばす」ことの大切さが重要なテーマだった。知識を増やすより「自分らしさ」を見出して伸ばす時間を持たせようと「**ゆとり教育**」も行われた。だが、それが**学力低下**に繋がっているのではないかとの批判も出て、現在、「ゆとり教育」は否定されているが、「個性を伸ばす」有効策が出ているわけではない。日本人の没個性的な性格、社会の**同調圧力**はなかなか修正されない。教育の専門家たちが手を焼いていることに、筆者が口を出すのはおこがましいが、多くの父兄が「学校教育」に期待し過ぎるように思う。学校が**課外（クラブ）活動**をやらせているだけで十分ではないか。むしろ家庭や地域活動の中で、大人た

ordered the darn Campari soda, though.

Politely speaking, Japanese are **cooperative** and follow the rules, and try to do the same as other people. The positive side of these characteristics will be shown when people have to line up for water at the time of natural disasters, or **form queues and ride on** public transportation such as trains and busses in an orderly manner. This kind of behavior would get many of that "Thumbs up!" chorus. But the flip side of Japanese characteristics might end up like the "Campari soda incident" that I wrote about earlier. We tend to feel comfortable if we do the same thing as others do **without thinking**. One's own "individuality" would be buried under the group mentality.

The Japanese educational circles have been aware of this, and the importance of "developing one's individuality" has been an essential theme for a long time. "***Yutori* education (a more relaxed education policy)**" has been done to find "one's own unique quality" and to make more time to encourage it rather than simply increasing knowledge. But after the criticism that "*Yutori* education" could be the cause of **declining academic achievement**, this more relaxed education policy was denied. Another answer to "develop one's individuality" hasn't yet been found. A lacking in personality, which is the characteristic

ちが、「自分らしく」あることや「個性を伸ばす」ことの“カッコ良さ”を実践して見せるのが近道なのではないだろうか？

世間や“お隣さん”とは違う言動をしても、他人に迷惑をかけず、「**我を通す**」のではないのなら尊重されることが子供に伝われば良いのである。「ちょっと変わっている。でも魅力的」というのが最大の賛辞になる身近な“小世界”が増えたらすばらしいと思う。「独立（independence）」した価値観を尊重しあう社会なら、「孤立（isolation）」することはない。実は、日本人は個々には面白い“変人”が多い。ディープな趣味を持つ人、地域の歴史に詳しい人、知られざる才能を持つ人、**波乱に富んだ半生**を過ごした人……。みんな十分に個性的で魅力的である。「孤立」を恐れて埋没させるのはもったいない。なお、私はもう「カンパリ・ソーダ」を呑まないことに決めている。

of Japanese people, and **peer pressure** by society are hard to change. I'm not a specialist in education, and I know that the teachers are trying their best to improve the current situation. But in my humble opinion, it seems that parents expect too much from the "school education." Isn't it good enough that the schools have **extracurricular activities** for the students? Isn't it a better and faster way to develop children's personality if adults can show them the coolness of being oneself at home and through local activities?

Parents can prove to them that they would be respected even when they act differently from their "neighbors" if it doesn't bother other people and if they are not **self-assertive**. That should be enough. I hope to see the world where the nicest compliment is something like, "It is a little bit different but attractive!" It would be nice to hear that often around us in Japan. If society respects the independent values of others, you won't become isolated. Surprisingly, if you see the Japanese people individually, there are many interesting and "strange" ones. A person who has a unique hobby and knows it very deeply, who knows very well about the local history, who has hidden abilities, who has had a **bumpy life**, and so on. They are unique and attractive. It's a pity if they hide their personalities for fear of "isolation." Oh, for what it's worth, I've decided not to order "Campari soda" at a restaurant anymore.

キーワード5● 行動ファースト

「弱者」に寄り添う方法を身につける

日本を含む東洋文化圏には、「**惻隠の情**」という言葉がある。孔子と並ぶ儒教の偉人・**孟子**の「惻隠の心は仁の端なり」という言葉が元になっている。現代語に訳せば、「困っている人に同情（compassion）することは、立派な人格になる最初の段階だ」というもの。人間の善良さを信じた哲学者らしい言葉である。

キリスト教には「善きサマタリアン」の話が『**新約聖書**』に出てくる。旅人が強盗に襲われて道端に倒れていた。そこに通りかかった最初のユダヤ人祭司も、次の律法学者も彼を救わなかった。3人目のサマリア人だけが助けた。イエスが説く「隣人愛」の隣人とは「善きサマリア人たれ」ということだ。ここから、「災難や急病の人を、**居合わせた人**（bystander）が無償かつ善意で救おうとした場合、結果の責任を問われない」という法律（Good Samaritan law）が、米国やカナダに生まれた。

イスラム教でもムスリムの果たすべき「**五行**」のひとつとして、困窮者を助けるための義務的な喜捨を「ザカート（zakat）」、自発的な**喜捨**を「サダカ（sadaqa）」と呼んで重視する。本来の意味は「（自身の）浄め」だ。……この

Learn to care for the weak

In the Oriental cultural area including Japan, there is an expression ***sokuin no jō* (compassion)**. It came from the words by **Mencius**, a great philosopher in Confucianism along with Confucius. The translation would mean, "Having compassion for the people in trouble is the first step to become a better person." He believed in the essential goodness of man.

In Christianity, there is a story of the "Good Samaritan" in the **New Testament**. A man was attacked by robbers and left on the road half dead. A Jewish priest, who happened to be going down the same road, didn't save him. Then, a Levite passed by, but he didn't save the man, either. The third man was a Samaritan, and he helped the man. What Jesus meant by "Love of our neighbor" is "Be a good Samaritan." "Good Samaritan law" was born in the U.S. and Canada according to this teaching. It is legal protection to **bystanders** who assist, in good faith, and without pay, to those who are injured or ill.

In Islam, as one of the **Five Pillars of Islam**, Muslims are encouraged to make **contributions** to the poor; an obligatory charity is zakat, and a voluntary charity is sadaqa. The original meaning of the words is

ように世界には「人類愛（love for humanity）」と呼ぶものが普遍的にある。おそらく未来にも続く普遍性だ。

ちょっと前置きが長くなったが、この人類ならではの愛をベースにした普遍的な価値観および行動が、これからはますます重視されることを、まず知って欲しい。念頭にあるのは、さまざまなハラスメントを受けている弱い立場の人々である。学校でのいじめ被害児童、DV被害者、**謂れのない差別を受けている人**、耐えがたい**因習**を強いられる人でもある。それだけではない。上司たちが、あるいは組織ぐるみで、商業道徳に反し、反社会的なことをしているのを知りながら沈黙するしかない立場にある人も含めたい。

時代は、こうした弱い立場の人の声に耳を傾ける方向に向いているように思う。私だけの、**そそっかしい**判断だろうか？

日本には「**長いものには巻かれよ**」、「泣く子と地頭には勝てぬ」、「泣き寝入り」などの哀しくて嫌な言葉があるが、21世紀はこれらを「**死語**」として葬るべき時代なのだ。弱い立場にある人に寄り添い、助け合うための方法、

"purification (of oneself)." As you could see here, there is something universal called "love for humanity" in the world. It is a universality that will continue to exist in the future as well.

This introduction has become a little too long, but what I'd like you to know, first of all, is that these universal values and actions based on the love of humanity will be highly regarded increasingly from now on. What I'm talking about is the weak who are getting all sorts of harassment; Children bullied at school, victims of domestic violence, **people discriminated against for no apparent reason**, people who are forced to follow unbearable, **old customs**, and many more. I'd like to include the people who are forced to remain silent about the fact that their superiors or the whole organization are doing something antisocial against the business ethics.

Luckily, it seems that the time is changing in the direction where society will listen to the voice of people who are in vulnerable positions. Do you think it's **too soon** to tell?

In Japan, we have sad and horrible expressions such as "**If you can't beat them, join them**." "It is no more possible to beat city hall than to reason with a whining child." "Grin and bear it." In the 21st century, we have

組織化のノウハウ、勝つための戦略的訓練が必要だ。モラルを大切にする企業人なら**内部告発**を、親会社の値下げ圧力や**賄賂**要求に悩む**下請け**は断固たる拒否を、雇い止めや労基法違反には訴訟を……。すみやかな行動によって、暗闇を払えば、日本および日本人は、世界から本当に尊敬される国になると思う。

to bury these expressions as "**dead words**." What we need is to be compassionate to the weak, a method to help each other, know-how to form an organization, and strategic training to win. If you are a business person with a strong sense of justice, become a **whistleblower**. If you are **subcontractor** getting pressure for a discount or demand for **bribes** from the parent company, refuse it firmly. If your contract is terminated, or if you find something that is against the Labor Standards Act, sue the company. Japan and the Japanese will become a country and people respected by the world if we act fast to fight against the dark pressure in society.

終わりに

日本に外国人観光客が増えていると本文で何度も書いた。政府が目標とする「**2020年までに4000万人**」というのも大きすぎる目標ではない。しかし、その内訳を見れば、増えているのはほとんど東南アジアの、急速に経済力をつけた国々である。米国やオーストラリアも増えているのは、これら**経済成長圏の国々**と関わりを持つ人が増えたことの余波だ。彼らにとって、日本は数ある旅行先の「One of Them」に過ぎない。より魅力的な観光地が見つかれば、どんどんそちらにシフトして行くだろう。

訪日外国人がもらす不満で多いのは、「日本人が英語を話せない」ことだ。これが私にはよくわからない。現在、60歳代後半から70歳にかけての高齢者（「**団塊世代**」）でも、高校への進学率は約64%にも達したのだから、英語は丸6年以上学習しているはずだ。それ以降の世代なら大学進学率も上昇したので、もっと長く英語に接している。少なくとも「アイハバ・アナッポーペン（I have an apple and pen）」が理解できることはピコ太郎の「PPAP」が証明しているではないか。「理解できない、話せない」振りをしているだけで、本当は「理解しているが話さない」のではないだろうか？　カタカナですぐに**和製英語**を作るの

Conclusion

As I wrote several times in this book, the number of foreign tourists has been increasing in Japan. The Japanese government has a target of "**40 million tourists by the year 2020**," and this is not overly ambitious. But when we look closely at the information about the tourists, the increased number of people are mostly coming from Southeast Asian countries whose economic power is rapidly getting stronger. Also, the number of tourists from the U.S. and Australia is increasing, which is the effect of the connections that people have with those **economically growing countries**. For them, Japan is just one of the many tourist spots. If they find a more attractive place, they will change their destinations without hesitation.

The number one complaint from the inbound tourists is the fact that the Japanese people can't speak English. I don't understand this. Even the elderly people between late sixties and seventies (**baby boomers**) must have studied English for more than six years because the high school entrance rate was as high as 64% then. The generation after that must have learned English longer than that as its university entrance rate went up. The fact that they can at least understand PIKOTARO's PPAP (I have an apple and pen…) proves that they can understand English to some extent. My guess is they

も、基礎的な理解ができていなければ無理だろう……。でも、もうそんな振りで「お茶を濁す」ことはできない。

経済成長圏の国々では英語は**準公用語**になりつつある。バイリンガルを武器とする若い世代は、自分の才能を伸ばすことに貪欲だ。医師や弁護士、博士号の資格取得、国際機関への就職、世界的大企業への就職などに果敢に挑戦している。必要なら新たに第三、第四の言語も習得しようとする。すべては伸び盛りの自国と自分に役立たせたいからだろう。実際、彼らは世界のどこに行っても、**先人**たちが築いた強固な拠点と**人脈**があるから、怖れることを知らない。

経済活動の縮小、少子高齢化、**中核都市への人口集中**……かつての大国ニッポンは、沈みゆく太陽のように国力を衰退させている。志向が**内向き**になっているのに、一時的な観光客増加に浮かれていたら、本当に消滅してしまう。**時代に合わない**価値観や意識を変えないと「ヤバイ！」のである。そんな**危機感**を持ちつつ、現代ニッポンを呪縛し規制している力を「曖昧なタブー」ととらえ、身近な視点から多角的に検討を加えてみたのが本書である。

are just pretending that they "can't understand or speak English" while they "can understand but can't speak English" in reality. Japanese people have been making "**Japanese English**" words in katakana Japanese characters. But if we can't understand the basic English, it would have been difficult to do that. Anyway, we can't continue to pretend that we can't speak English.

In the emerging countries, English is becoming the **second national language**. Bilingual young people are eager to develop their talents. They are bravely challenging to become a doctor or lawyer, to obtain a Ph.D., to get a job at an international organization or big global company. If necessary, they are willing to learn a third or fourth language. They do everything for their developing countries and for themselves. In fact, wherever they go in the world, there are strong bases and **human networks** built by the **previous immigrants**. So, they aren't afraid of going abroad.

Shrinking economic activities, a falling birth rate and an aging population, a **population concentration in core cities** … Japan used to be an economic power house, but its power is getting weak like the sun setting in the sea. We have to be aware that Japan is becoming **introverted**. If we simply get too excited about the temporary increase of the inbound tourists, Japan would disappear for sure. It is critical that we change

そして最後の章では、私らしくもない「**上から目線**」で、日本人がこれからタブーと正面から向き合うべきことを書いてしまった。

私たち高齢者に残された時間は20年もないだろう。日本の蘇生を見届けるには時間が足りない。若い世代に**後事を託す**しかないのだが、アドバイスできるとしたら、「国を背負う必要はない。まず、世界を舞台に自分を輝かせてほしい」ということ。そうなれば、コスモポリタンとしての意識が全体に高まり、世界で業績を重ねるグローバル人材が輩出するだろう。経済を支えるのも海外で稼ぐ方法しかないようだ。今のステージは少し狭すぎる。

日本人の美質がずば抜けていることは疑いがない。**先人**たちに敬意を払い、自信を持って踏み出してほしいと思う。なんだか、**遺言**みたいになってしまったので、ここで筆を置く。

土屋　晴仁

our values or our ways of thinking that are **outdated**. With this **sense of crisis** in mind, I described the power that is restricting and regulating present-day Japan as "ambiguous taboos," and tried to analyze them from various point of views in this book. In the last section, although it's not my **style to patronize the reader**, I anyhow wrote that the Japanese people should stand against the taboos.

It would be probably less than 20 years left that elderly people like me could live. It wouldn't be enough time for us to see the revival of Japan. So, we have to **leave the work** to the younger generation. If I could give one piece of advice to them, that would be, "You don't have to be burdened with your country. First, go abroad and be the best you can be over there." That way, the younger generation will be able to build up a sense of cosmopolitan, and many people will be able to achieve great things globally. To support Japanese economy, the only possible way would be to earn money in other countries. The current stage is too small for them.

There is no doubt that the Japanese are a people of great virtue. I want them to pay respect to the **people in front of them**, and step forward with confidence. Well, it's getting to sound like a **farewell note**. It's time for me to stop writing here.

Haruhito Tsuchiya

[対訳ニッポン双書]

現代日本のタブー
その余りにもビミョーな存在

Taboos of Present-day Japan: The Exquisite Subtleness of Being

2018年7月8日　第1刷発行

著　者　土屋 晴仁

発行者　浦　晋亮

発行所　IBCパブリッシング株式会社
〒162-0804 東京都新宿区中里町29番3号 菱秀神楽坂ビル9F
Tel. 03-3513-4511　Fax. 03-3513-4512
www.ibcpub.co.jp

印刷所　株式会社シナノパブリッシングプレス

ISBN978-4-7946-0545-0